IN THE

SHADOW

OF

TENNIS LEGENDS

THE *Lenny Simpson* STORY

LENNY
SIMPSON

with Bethany Bradsher

ISBN: 979-8-218-09576-5

Cover and interior design by Stephanie Whitlock Dicken.

Contents

Dedication

To Mom, who instilled in me a deep faith and reliance on God.
Her sacrifice to give me the opportunity at such a young age to
follow my dream was enormous. I'm forever thankful for that.

To Jo Ann, who has stood by me side for the last 49 ½ wonderful years.
Thank you for always supporting me and encouraging me
to reach for my dreams. You are an amazing mom and
grandmother and the love of my life. I thank God for you.

—ᴍ—

Foreword

BY JOHNNIE ASHE

A few years ago I was at the U.S. Open for Arthur Ashe Kids Day, an annual event organized in memory of my older brother Arthur. Lenny Simpson and a group of his One Love kids were there leading stroke demonstrations and participating in the festivities. I was in the President's Box and I saw one of Lenny's tennis students looking around with a lost expression on her face. She locked in on me, probably because I was the only other black face in the room, but I knew she was looking for Lenny.

"Coach Lenny had to go out for a minute," I told her. "He'll be right back. What do you think of Coach Lenny?"

"Hmmm," she replied. "I wish he was my dad."

That exchange tells you everything you need to know about the influence of Lenny Simpson, one of my oldest friends in the game. Lenny and I met when we were ten or eleven years old and training with Dr. R. Walter Johnson at his ATA Junior Development Program in Lynchburg, Va. If one of us realized all of our socks were dirty, the other one would share his clean ones. We traveled to tournaments together, competed on Dr. Johnson's backyard court and tried our best to behave in his strict program.

When I joined the Marine Corps at age seventeen and served two tours in Vietnam, Lenny and I lost touch. We connected when Arthur became ill in 1988 and again at his funeral five years later, but we didn't truly rekindle our friendship until he was inducted into the N.C. Tennis Hall of Fame in 2011. I introduced him at that ceremony, which was a significant milestone in itself, but the other moment that stands out to me is a conversation we had at breakfast the morning of the induction.

As we ate, I said to Lenny, "Time to go home now." And he replied, "I'm thinking about it." We both sensed that God was directing him back to Wilmington, even though we couldn't have known that his return home would lead to the amazing opportunity to buy and restore Dr. Eaton's home and tennis court where Lenny had held his first tennis racket.

I so wish that my brother Arthur had lived long enough to see what Lenny created for the kids of Wilmington, N.C. Lenny and Arthur, his "big brother" from those days in Dr. Johnson's summer program, shared a conviction that their tennis success gave them a platform to give back. When Lenny first called to tell me about the creation of One Love Tennis, I asked him what I could do to help, and the next call I made was to Head. The tennis equipment company agreed to sell rackets and balls to Lenny's program at a drastically reduced cost. I know that Arthur would have made that phone call for Lenny if he could have, and whenever possible I have tried to support him in the same way my brother would have.

Lenny was a talented tennis player, and because he is such a people person he was always a success as a tennis pro. But his latest chapter, which has allowed him to pour a lifetime of hard lessons and triumphs into a program that will teach children values and perspective through the sport he loves, is his best chapter. Lenny is making sure that the One Love children know all about the history of black players in tennis, players like my brother Arthur. I'm grateful that through this book, the world will appreciate his important role in that history.

—⚉—

Foreword

BY KATRINA ADAMS

This book is called *In The Shadow of Tennis Legends,* but I actually came up through the tennis world in the shadow of Lenny Simpson's legend. Lenny's reputation as a tough player and a winner preceded him, and as an NCAA doubles champion in 1987 and a winner of 20 WTA doubles titles in the '80s and '90s, I was standing on the shoulders of Lenny and his friends who toppled so many barriers for black players in the sport.

I knew about Lenny's success as a player and a coach, and I always respected him from afar, but we didn't get to know each other well until he moved back to his hometown of Wilmington and started One Love Tennis. In 2014, a few months before I became the first black president of the U.S. Tennis Association, I reconnected with Lenny and Jo Ann when they brought some of their One Love kids to Flushing Meadows for Arthur Ashe Kids Day at the U.S. Open.

I fell in love with the kids and the mission of One Love, and I stayed in touch with Lenny and saw them again at the U.S. Open after I took over the USTA in 2015. Soon, thanks to Lenny's commitment to educating young players about the history of the sport, a group of kids had written heartfelt letters asking for official USTA recognition of Althea Gibson. When I came to Wilmington in 2017 to speak at a One Love fundraising event, they presented me with piles of letters in person. I remember one little girl writing, "Even if it's just a hot dog stand, something needs to be named for Althea."

This groundswell from the young tennis players of Wilmington re-ignited a fire in me to help push for a prominent and appropriate memorial to the great Althea Gibson. Armed with the letters from the One Love kids, I worked to keep the idea at the forefront until finally, in the fall of 2019, the statue of

Althea was unveiled at Flushing Meadows. Lenny and Jo Ann and a group of their kids were there, celebrating the recognition that might never have become a reality without their advocacy.

That moment represented a full-circle moment for Lenny, who was handed his first tennis racket by a young Althea Gibson way back in 1953. But that statue dedication wouldn't have happened if Lenny had ignored God's call to move back to his hometown and make a difference for kids there in the same way Dr. Eaton made a difference for him. In the most profound full-circle moment of all, Lenny and Jo Ann are influencing kids from the very same tennis court where Lenny received that racket from Althea so many decades ago. It's like the plot of an inspirational movie, but it's Lenny's real-life story because of his dedication to helping others grow through the game that gave him so much.

If Lenny had just retired quietly from his career as a tennis pro and stayed in Tennessee, he still would have represented a powerful legacy in tennis. But because he has dedicated most of the past decade to the kids of his hometown and they are out making their own change in the world, that legacy will keep sending out ripples long after all of us are gone. I'm extraordinarily grateful to be a witness of that powerful legacy—to celebrate the impact of the man who was one of my own personal tennis legends.

In 2018 Dr. R. Walter Johnson's court in Lynchburg, Va., where I spent every summer of my life from age nine to eighteen, was renovated and dedicated. I attended the ceremony along with Johnnie Ashe, left, and Katrina Adams, right, since we were all beneficiaries of Dr. Johnson's coaching and discipline.

Introduction

The black tennis players of today stand on the shoulders of so many pioneers, but there are four faces that would be carved on the Mount Rushmore of black American tennis. Incredibly, it was my great privilege to learn about the sport, and about life, from all four of these giants. I can't conceive of how diminished my life would have been if I had not crossed paths with Althea Gibson, Dr. Hubert Eaton, Dr. R. Walter Johnson and Arthur Ashe. I have been uniquely blessed, and I feel thankful every day for their influence on me.

Althea Gibson blazed a singular trail in our sport, becoming the first black player to take a singles Grand Slam title in 1956 and then capturing four more in the next two years. Her talent and courage have become the stuff of legend; when she cleared every major hurdle in amateur tennis and found few financial prospects in women's pro tennis, she changed sports entirely and became the first African-American woman to join the LPGA. She left an outsized legacy, to be sure, but she was also the person who spoke glorious words of possibility to me when I was only five years old and then, for the next few years, took the time to coach me through the fundamentals of tennis. Althea planted a seed in me that is still, sixty-five years later, producing fruit.

I might have missed out on my life's calling completely if I had grown up in a different section of Wilmington, North Carolina, but because I had the good fortune to live behind Dr. Hubert Eaton, I was exposed to a world of tennis that captivated and transformed me, a world first introduced to me by my next-door neighbor, a talented tennis player named Mr. Nat Jackson. A championship tennis player himself, Dr. Eaton fought for development and opportunity of black players throughout his life, both in the city where he lived and practiced medicine and throughout the nation. Somehow, between caring for patients and working tirelessly for civil rights in Wilmington, he coached countless tennis players on his backyard court, since black players weren't permitted to play anywhere else. Mr. Jackson invited me into that world, and Dr. Eaton was a powerful mentors on and off the tennis court whose commitment to tennis and the greater good altered the course of my life.

Dr. R. Walter Johnson's nickname, "Whirlwind," was appropriate, because the man never stopped. Johnson first made his name as a star college football player and college football coach, and then as a top physician in Lynchburg, Va. But like his friend and fellow crusader Dr. Eaton, he was committed to identifying and cultivating talented black tennis players. He also built a tennis facility at his home to serve young players who were shut out because of segregation, and his courts became home for the only junior development tennis program in the nation for black athletes. Lynchburg became my spring and summer home when I was just nine years old, and because Dr. Johnson took an interest in me I was exposed to a wealth of competitive tennis opportunities and lifelong friendships forged during those warm months in Virginia.

During my first stay in Lynchburg I was homesick and uncertain, and Dr. Johnson was wise enough to assign me an older mentor. That was the beginning of one of the most important friendships of my life with a true tennis legend—Arthur Ashe. The only black man ever to win the singles titles at Wimbledon, the U.S. Open, and the Australian Open, Ashe was an unforgettable player who left a humanitarian legacy that went way past the game and changed the nation indelibly in his forty-nine short years. I had the privilege of serving as a pallbearer and speaking at his funeral, and I still miss him every day.

The top film at the Academy Awards in 1995 was Forrest Gump, a movie beloved for its unique storytelling and Tom Hanks' endearing portrayal of its title character. The most unique aspect to Forrest's story arc is the fact that he was connected in some way to every significant event throughout three decades of American history—John F. Kennedy's presidency, The Vietnam War, the Watergate scandal and more. Forrest covered much more ground than I did, but when you consider the world of black tennis from the 1940sx to the 1990s you'll see that I have a little bit of Forrest Gump in me.

There would be no story of black tennis's growth and integration in the U.S. without Althea, Dr. Eaton, Mr. Jackson, Dr. Johnson and Arthur, and I had the immense privilege of crossing paths in a significant way with each one of them. Just as the sport's landscape would be impossible to sketch without these five pillars of tennis, my own story would be a mere shadow of what it became if I had never crossed paths with them. God saw fit to give me meaningful friendships with these five, and I'm endlessly grateful. As my own story unfolds, I'll return to them in more detail because not only are their lives integral to my own, they are also each extraordinary in their own right and deserve to be remembered and celebrated.

—◊—

CHAPTER ONE
Roots

In the year that I was born, my parents bought a plot of land from Dr. Hubert Eaton, a young physician and a nationally ranked tennis player. Dr. Eaton, who was committed to investing his time and money to improving life for the black citizens of Wilmington, North Carolina, owned nearly everything in the neighborhood. My parents didn't know him at the time, but some of my family members already lived nearby, and my mom and dad wanted a house in the growing city that would accommodate their growing family.

My father and grandfather, who were both contractors and carpenters, built our house at 1417 Ann Street, which was finished in time for my mother to bring me home there after my birth on September 23, 1948.

Both of my parents considered Wilmington the big city; my mom grew up in nearby Burgaw, and my dad came from an even smaller town called Long Creek. In addition to building houses, my paternal grandfather was a minister who pastored a church in Long Creek, and when I was growing up people compared me to him all the time. I became accustomed to hearing that I would probably be a minister too, because I was so much like my grandfather.

Seeking more opportunity for my father and his contractor business, my parents moved into their new home in Wilmington, but my mom kept her teaching job in Burgaw until I was in the fifth grade. I was raised inside a school from the time I was three years old. Most days, I would either go to school in Burgaw with my mom or to the school in Hampstead where my Aunt Ruth was a teacher. Of course, I was expected to behave, since I was related to the teacher. When I started kindergarten myself, I still went to Burgaw with my mom to attend school there, and in the second grade she was officially my teacher, even though she had been teaching me for my whole life.

Eventually my mom got a position in Wilmington—at Peabody School on the north side of town and I moved to that school along with my sister Helenda, who was five years younger than me. But for a decade or so, she and a couple of other women who taught in Pender County got up early every single day to carpool the thirty miles to their jobs. My mom never once complained. She loved her job; she was good at it and she knew it was a very nice position for a woman in the 1950s.

My father quickly built a reputation in Wilmington as one of the best carpenters and bricklayers in the area. Not only did he build our house, but he also built many of the houses in our neighborhood, for white and black people alike. My father was talented and a hard worker, and he should have had his own construction company. He could have been a rich man if he had the same opportunities as a white man in his profession, but he kept his head down to provide for us and helped the heart of downtown Wilmington rise up out of the dirt in the process. I'll never forget the day my mom and I walked downtown to bring my dad lunch when he was working on the big Belk-Beery building downtown. It was a showpiece and one of the most impressive buildings on Front Street, and I was so proud that my daddy was helping it become a reality.

If my father had been given the professional opportunities he deserved in the construction business life would have been different for me; I could have been part of a successful, multigenerational business rather than just watching my dad search for jobs from others. He couldn't pass down those type of advantages, but he did pass down a determination and work ethic that has served me throughout my life. He was a good provider and my sister and I had what we needed, even if my father never really expressed his affections or his feelings to us. My father was a hard man who grew up in a time and a culture when men didn't share their feelings. His father didn't express his emotions either, and my dad never saw any other way when he was growing up. I understood much later that he and my mother were struggling in their marriage, but he did what he needed to do to help us make ends meet and to live in a nice house in a stable, middle-class neighborhood.

My parents were all about discipline, and my mother took the lead in administering that discipline when I stepped out of line. She used to make me go out and cut my own switches for the forthcoming whipping, but even when she was hard on me her love for me was evident, and I always understood that she would sacrifice anything to help pave the way for my sister and I to have opportunities. She was wholly committed to our education in the academic sense, but her first priority was laying the foundation of our faith. We grew up going to church, hearing my mom quote scripture and understanding that our faith in God would be a source of constant strength no matter what we faced. Every time we were on the verge of a new experience and we were uncertain, my mom would remind us of Psalm 27:1: "The Lord is my light and my salvation; whom shall I fear? The Lord is the stronghold of my life; of whom shall I be afraid?" It's a truth that has given me courage more times than I can possibly count.

If I ever committed an infraction that my mom didn't happen to witness, she could rely on her number one neighborhood spy, her sister and my Aunt Ruth. Aunt Ruth lived right on the corner of Ann Street and 14th Street, and her backyard overlooked the big field that Dr. Eaton had turned into a park for us neighborhood kids. Aunt Ruth could see every single that went on in that vacant lot, and since she never had children of her own she made me her special project.

The other kids and I were always getting in little fights back there, and when Aunt Ruth saw me throwing punches she would come out and watch it play out, and then she would have a talk with me. She didn't immediately forbid me from fighting; instead, she would give me a talk about standing up for myself when it was necessary. If she saw me letting other kids take advantage of me, or picking on younger kids for no reason, she would grab me by the ear and pull me home, where she would talk to me about the importance of taking care of myself. She had a cocker spaniel that she treated like a child, and every night she and her dog would walk my sister and me home, giving us advice the whole way.

Some of my strongest childhood memories, and the moments that lay the spiritual foundation of my life, happened out at my maternal grandparents' property in Burgaw. In the years before my grandparents moved to Wilmington when I was five, I used to spend large portions of my summer months out there with them, and it was there that I started to get glimpses of my grandmother's deep Christian faith and wisdom. As young as I was, I listened to Mama Henny (as everyone called her) intently because I knew that she had understanding about the Lord forged through decades of prayer and trials. She was always teaching me, always demonstrating ways that God should be present in every aspect of life.

My grandparents had a few acres of land on which they had planted a variety of vegetables, and every day we would go out into Mama Henny's garden to pick corn, collards, butterbeans, or whatever was ripe for harvest that day, and as she worked she would weave her faith and her favorite verses into act of gardening, or the weather, or any aspect of the day. Her life was a sermon. While we picked vegetables, my hard-working grandfather was working the land with just a mule and a plow, getting a plot ready for the next round of planting. And when my grandfather wasn't working on the farm, he was likely to take me on a walk. Those walks are another part of my young life I could never forget, mostly because they wore me out. We walked and walked and walked down one country road, four or five miles at a time. They didn't have a car, so walking was the only way my grandparents got around, but I thought he was going to walk me to death when I was little. I understand now that he was showing his love for me, by spending so much time with me.

Later we would go on our marathon walks with my sister Helenda in a stroller, but before she was born it was often just me and my grandfather, who used the time to tell me stories and talk to me about his own faith. Both of my grandparents, in their own way, took plenty of time to speak into my life and set an example for how to live. He always told me about the watermelon man, and before long I was on perpetual lookout for the watermelon man to come by their house and sell us a watermelon. It was a huge highlight of my day.

We went to church with my grandmother several times a week, and my sister and I sang in the choir as soon as we were old enough. We went to sing for church services and all kinds of other occasions, and I went with her so often I usually didn't know exactly what the service was for. But one day, when I was about ten years old, I was standing up there next to my grandmother singing, and I looked down and got the shock of my life. There, in an open coffin, was the watermelon man! I was so surprised I couldn't stay quiet. I shouted out, "Mama Henny! That's the watermelon man!" I didn't even know we were going to a funeral, and I certainly didn't know it was the funeral of a famous local person like him.

My grandmother was so incredibly influential, and not just on me and my sister. She was undeniably the rock of our extended family. Everyone came to her seeking advice or bringing a prayer request; they knew that this devoted lady's prayers were righteous and effective. Through every challenge and opportunity that I would embrace in the future, I knew that my grandmother and my mother were praying fervently for me. They prayed for success and humility on the tennis court, for success in the classroom, for patience through the trials we faced when traveling through a segregated South to tennis tournaments. Their prayers sustained me and my sister, who suffered from various health problems, through countless difficult situations.

When my grandmother passed away in 1984 at the age of eighty-nine, my mother became the prayer warrior, the backbone of the family. She learned from the best how to, in the words of Proverbs 3:5-6, *"Trust in the Lord with all your heart, and lean not on your own understanding. In all your ways acknowledge Him, and He will make your paths straight."* Through these saints in my own family, I learned to rely on God completely no matter what. He has always been faithful; He has been the light of my life and has proven Himself trustworthy even through dark times. I can't imagine my life without the grace of Jesus or the light of God's word.

—⁓—

CHAPTER 2

A Mystery

I don't have too many vivid memories on Ann Street until I was five years old, and I started to notice the mysterious comings and goings of my next-door neighbor, Mr. Nathaniel Jackson. I wasn't permitted to leave my yard, but I loved to climb up in the big old oak tree in front of our house, and from that perch I could watch what was going on up and down my block. One afternoon I spotted Mr. Jackson leaving the house, walking down the street and around the corner, out of spying distance. The most intriguing part of this, to young Lendward, was his clothes. He wore white shoes, white socks, white shorts, and a white shirt and carried a wooden contraption I had never seen before. It wasn't exactly common, in the late '40s, to see a black man walking around Wilmington in a spotless all-white outfit.

Before long I realized that a couple of hours later, Mr. Jackson came home, always carrying a cold bottle of Coca-Cola. Well, if I was fascinated by his daily routine before because of his attire, I was completely transfixed because of those Cokes. They looked delicious, I was hot up in that tree, and I was dying to know where he was getting them. I learned to time my other activities around Mr. Jackson's daily walks to and from his house. I didn't have a watch, but if I did I could have set it by the moment when Mr. Jackson walked out his front door and around the corner. I might have been inside having a snack or playing, but I would bolt out the door at the appointed time. More than once my puzzled parents asked, "Lendward, why are you in such a hurry to go outside?" I would say, "I have to go meet Mr. Jackson." They didn't ask more questions. I was only five, and I guess they figured my daily habits weren't too interesting.

Mr. Jackson was a family friend, and my parents knew all about the mysterious world around the corner that he was entering every afternoon.

But they weren't tennis players, and they couldn't have possibly understood how deeply curious I was about the man in white with his cold glass bottles of soda. For weeks I stayed in the safety of my oak tree, spying and wondering, until finally one day I couldn't take it anymore. Gathering my courage, I called out from my leafy hiding place:

"Hey, where did you get that Coca-Cola from?"

"Right around the corner, at the tennis court," Mr. Jackson answered. "If your mom would let me take you around there, I could show you."

Well, that's where I hit a major roadblock. Mr. Jackson knew, and I knew, that my mom wasn't going to be willing to let me go over to the tennis court with him. It wasn't that she didn't trust Mr. Jackson, and Dr. Eaton was our family doctor so she certainly didn't have any problem with him or his family. She would say "no" because she didn't want me to get in the way of the adults. In my mom's view of the world, children needed to keep quiet and mind their manners, and barging into a tennis match meant for grown-ups was completely out of the question.

I knew this was true, but it didn't keep me from trying. To be honest, I had no idea was tennis was at first and I wasn't that interested in hanging out with a bunch of adults, but the Coca-Cola was enticing, and I was bored. So I asked my mom if I could go over to the Eatons' with Mr. Jackson. Predictably, she shut the idea down immediately. I kept persisting, and I realized as the weeks went by that I really, really, wanted to be allowed to go. Part of my eagerness had to do with the fact that my mom was determined to refuse, since we're always more intrigued by the forbidden. And as I became more interested, I made an important shift from the front yard to the backyard, and that's when my undercover spying operation kicked into gear.

When I ventured into my backyard on one of those warm afternoons, I heard exciting sounds floating over the bushes. I could hear balls bouncing, people laughing and shouting, and strange combinations of numbers being called out. Dr. Eaton's tennis court wasn't directly behind my house, but it was just one yard over, so I realized that I could slip between the hedges, crawl on my belly for seventy-five feet, and soon I would be on the edge of the court. What I saw there simply amazed me. I had never witnessed anything so exciting in my young life; as far as I was concerned, I was living just adjacent to Disneyworld.

There was my neighbor Mr. Jackson in his sparkling white outfit, along with a bunch of other grown-ups similarly dressed in white. They each had what I was calling a "thingamajig" in their hand, and some traded shots across the net while others watched. They were invested in what they were doing, but they laughed and teased each other easily even while they worked up a sweat trying to come out on top. I was completely swept up by all of it: the competition, the intensity, the fun, and the bottles of Coca-Cola that the losing player had to buy for everyone else at the end of each day's play.

I tried to make myself small and silent, and since I viewed the world as a five-year-old I was convinced that if I felt like I was invisible behind those bushes I really *was* invisible. I had found an easy pathway to a world that fascinated me endlessly, and since I was so good at spying, I reasoned, no one would ever know I was there watching.

Except, of course, for the fact that *everyone* knew I was there watching. I wasn't nearly as subtle as I thought I was. Dr. Eaton, Mr. Jackson and their friends at the court had spotted me but chosen to keep it to themselves. Mr. Jackson had quietly been an advocate for me through those months, asking my mom himself if she would be willing to let me visit the court with him. But my mom, as you might have already figured out, was not easily swayed.

So I kept up my sneaky daily ritual through the backyard bushes and, whenever I thought the wind might have changed in my household, lobbying my mom again and being rebuffed again. Dr. Eaton had even installed lights on his court, so I remember lying in my bed many times, unable to sleep because I could hear tennis balls hitting the clay—my mind spinning images of my new neighborhood heroes playing the sport I was learning to love from my dark bedroom and my cramped, leafy daytime vantage point.

—⚊—

My mother and I in all of our Easter finery.

CHAPTER 3

Mr. Jackson

Nathaniel Jackson was the very first tennis player I ever encountered. He was one of my heroes, because he took the time to take a little boy under his wing and invite him to the hallowed ground of Dr. Eaton's tennis court. His generosity and kindness were enough to make him exceptional, but I had no idea, back when I was quizzing him about where he came by his cold Coca-Cola, that I was living next door to one of the top American tennis players of the past thirty years.

Let me say this right up front: I played with Arthur Ashe and Althea Gibson, and through my years in the game I encountered many, many talented athletes. But in his heyday, Nat Jackson could have beaten them all. He was an unbelievable force on the tennis court, and he was in his forties by the time I met him. He was a package player—tenacious, heady, creative in his shot choices. He was a master of the art of "chip and charge," an early style of play at the net that has virtually disappeared from today's game.

Born in Laurinburg, N.C. in 1912, Nathaniel learned to play tennis alongside his brother Franklyn, and he made his first national impression when he was just seventeen and won the 1929 American Tennis Association Junior National Championship. (The ATA is the official governing body of black tennis.) He was the top junior again in 1930, and after that he and Franklyn proceeded to take the ATA doubles world by storm. The two Jacksons won the ATA National Doubles Championship in 1931, 1933, 1934, 1935, 1936 and 1938, and in 1934 Mr. Jackson also won the Singles Championship.

There's no doubt in my mind that Mr. Jackson would have been unstoppable if he had been permitted to play against white opponents. His name would be known as a tennis star worldwide, not just among those who followed the segregated game. As a young man he made his home in Wilmington and befriended Dr. Eaton, who became his opponent many times. In the early days, they had to play on the only courts available to black tennis players—the old rundown public courts on South Tenth Street—and later they upgraded to playing at Dr. Eaton's backyard facility. By the time he was making his daily treks around the corner to Orange Street and piquing my five-year-old curiosity, he had mostly retired from ATA competition and was breaking another type of barrier in Wilmington as the city's first black postal carrier.

It was a very important and sought-after job, since so few good government positions were available for black people in Wilmington during that time. It's likely that his tennis friendships, with professionals like Dr. Eaton and Mr. George Norman, who was the city employment director, helped open that door for Mr. Jackson. In the same way that white businesspeople in the city gathered on the golf courses and tennis courts of their country clubs to socialize and network, the tennis courts at 1406 Orange Street served that purpose for black professionals.

The personal and professional connections were a key element of those afternoons on the tennis court, but they didn't take away from the intense competition, culminating when the loser bought sodas for the winners. And even as he got older, Mr. Jackson was one of the strongest athletes out there, one of the players who usually got his Coca-Colas handed to him, rather than having to buy them himself. As I crouched underneath those bushes, trying to stay silent and undetected, I was watching some of the highest quality tennis being played by amateurs anywhere in the country.

The other players who frequented the court, friends of Dr. Eaton's who were beginners or novices, would play their matches earlier in the afternoon, but everyone knew that watching Mr. Jackson play was the main event. When he took his position on the court the chitchat would die down, because no one wanted to miss a shot. He was simply phenomenal, and even though the world missed the opportunity to see what he could do, those of us in Wilmington knew we were in the presence of something special.

I wasn't there on a legendary day in the late '50s when Mr. Jackson had the chance to go toe-to-toe with a world champion, but I heard plenty of stories that made me even more proud of my mentor. No media were present when Fred Perry stepped onto Dr. Eaton's court and played a friendly match against Mr. Jackson, but I know for a fact, friendly match or not, that Jackson proved that he would have held his own on any Grand Slam court with Perry. During the 1930s, the decade when Jackson was dominating the ATA circuit, Fred Perry was doing the same in the whites-only lawn tennis world. He won three straight Wimbledon titles from 1934 to 1936, and a large statue of him hitting his famous forehand drive still adorns the grounds of the All-England Club. In all, he claimed eight grand slam titles, and he was the first man to win all four (Wimbledon, the U.S. Open, the Australian Open and the French Open), although not in the same year.

Despite these many accomplishments, though, Fred Perry shared a common understanding with Nat Jackson of excelling in a sport that didn't accept you. While Jackson was excluded because of the color of his skin, Perry was allowed to compete but was never celebrated in his home country because of his working class background. Since many in the tennis world valued status and money over talent, Perry didn't get the respect he deserved in the U.K., and in the late '30s he moved to the U.S., playing on the pro circuit and eventually starting a clothing line.

For years, as I spent countless hours at 1406 Orange Street and much later oversaw the renovation of the house and tennis court, I had heard stories about the match between Perry and Jackson. I knew that Jackson had beaten Perry decisively, prompting Perry to say, "If Nathaniel Jackson had the same opportunities to play that I did, he would be in the top ten every year." I had even inherited a photo that I cherished of Dr. Eaton, Mr. Jackson, Fred Perry and an unknown fourth man. But it wasn't until 2019, when I was being honored at a United States Tennis Association awards banquet in Austin, when the final mystery of that day was revealed.

In God's providence, the USTA had assigned me a host named Jim Hendrix, and Jim mentioned that his father, Dr. John Hendrix, had been the tennis coach at Ohio State University and had a black friend in tennis who was also a doctor in North Carolina. Of course, I had a strong suspicion that I knew who John's doctor friend had been, and I also thought that I might be on the trail of identifying that unknown member of the Fred Perry foursome. He got back home to Columbus, Ohio, and he found the same photo that I had of the four men at Dr. Eaton's court. We were thrilled to discover that it was, in fact, his dad on the far left. Dr. Hendrix was a great friend of Perry, so Dr. Hendrix was there the day that two of tennis's unsung heroes played a rousing match hidden from the public eye.

I owe such an enormous debt to Mr. Jackson for his grace and generosity to an overly inquisitive, somewhat headstrong little boy. He didn't have to invite me into his neighborhood tennis refuge in the first place, and he certainly didn't need to lobby my mother repeatedly on my behalf. Eventually he would not only help teach me the game, but he would also urge others to teach me as well. I remember rainy days, when we couldn't work on tennis strokes at the court, when he would come to my house and coach me in my living room. Many a lamp was broken in that living room as I learned to perfect my strokes. We had a huge mirror on one wall of that room, and he would stand behind me and walk me through the proper strokes and footwork, over and over, showing me the right way to do it until it became second nature. I learned so much from Mr. Jackson, but because we became such close friends I also saw his struggles with alcohol, and the things I witnessed became a cautionary tale for me.

Mr. Jackson's drinking led to the end of his marriage and affected his relationship with his children, and so we helped take care of him. On many occasions I would deliver food to his house that my mom had prepared, or run to the corner store to get him an orange drink that soothed his stomach when it had been ravaged by alcohol abuse. I will always believe that the denial of Mr. Jackson's tennis dreams, his inability to compete on the international stage because of the color of his skin, frustrated him so much that he sought comfort in the bottle. I loved and respected him, but as I matured I also understood how destructive his drinking habit was and it made me so sad to see him deteriorate every day. I resolved to stay away from alcohol completely, and I've kept that promise to myself.

By giving me so much of his time and encouraging me, Mr. Jackson filled a void left by my father's stoicism. By taking such an eager interest in tennis and soaking up all of his coaching, I believe I filled a void for him as well. Because Mr. Jackson took the time to become my friend, he lifted the veil and let me into a magical new world — a world with tennis at its center. He's the unsung hero, not only of my story, but of a certain period in tennis history that too many people have forgotten.

I have the strong conviction that God laid out the cards of my life in an extraordinary way before I was born, and I just had to follow His navigation, like a treasure hunt with riches hidden along the way. One of the events that was certainly in the cards for me, something my parents might not have given much thought to at the time, was buying a lot next door to Nathaniel Jackson's house. Because he was my neighbor and he was the kind of man who would slow down to include a little boy perched in a tree, I was utterly changed.

—⁂—

In the late '50s three-time Wimbledon champion Fred Perry came to Dr. Eaton's court and played my mentor Mr. Nat Jackson. Here they are with Dr. Jim Hendrix.

CHAPTER 4

Breakthrough

I continued my junior secret agent routine for weeks—slipping out into the backyard, crawling through the bushes until I reached my vantage point adjacent to the tennis courts and trying to take in all of the tennis I could until I felt like I had been gone too long and my mom could be getting suspicious. But it should be no surprise, given my Aunt Ruth's propensity for knowing what I was up to and my poor efforts at invisibility, that word of my secret activities eventually got back to my mom.

She called me into her room one day and confronted me. "Lendward, you know I told you not to go over there. Now go on outside and cut some switches and tie them together." I always had to get my own switches for my whipping, and my mom was quick. Later, when I started having my own success on the tennis court, I would joke that the reason my footwork was so good was the years of practice I had trying to dodge my mama's switch. She finished the whipping, but before I left her room I had to try to explain why I was so determined.

I told her, "Mom, I love it over there. I'm not bothering anyone, and you may as well go ahead and punish me or whip me, because I want to go over there and I'm going to keep it up." And for a little while that's how it went: I went to the court every day, and I took my whipping when I got home. But one day, after she spanked me, my mom gave me the strangest look, and she said something I'll never forget. She told me, "If you're willing to keep getting punished like that over and over, this must be really important to you. I'm going to give you permission to go."

I was so excited! I caught up with Mr. Jackson that afternoon when he was returning from tennis and told him that I had finally been allowed to walk around the corner and through the gates with him, rather than sneaking through the backyard. He told me he would come by to pick me up the very next day, and I'm sure I didn't sleep well that night, especially with the sound of those tennis balls bouncing in and out of my dreams.

The next afternoon Mr. Jackson came to my door in his gleaming white outfit and took my hand as I stepped outside. I remember standing so tall as we walked; I hoped every person I knew in the neighborhood saw me on that short walk. But that was nothing compared to the amazement I felt when I finally stepped through the gates of 1406 Orange Street, at long last an invited guest to Disneyworld.

Everything seemed larger than life to my five-year-old eyes—the three-car garage, the immaculate grass and shrubs, the sprinkler system set up to keep the clay court watered, the lights that Dr. Eaton had installed for nighttime play. And there were wonders I had never beheld from my hiding place. There was a swimming pool! A ping-pong table and a pool table! You could have put that house and its amenities in any neighborhood in Wilmington and it would have been one of the nicest addresses there. For me, it was absolutely like stepping into another world.

There was always a crowd there for the afternoon matches, and that day Mr. Jackson walked me over to the court and introduced me to ten or eleven people, saving a tall young woman for last. He said, "And Lendward, this is Althea Gibson." I was too young to know why I should be impressed by Althea, but she had already made quite an impression in the tennis world. Her apex in the sport was still three years in the future, but when we met in 1953 Althea was ranked number seven in the world, she was in the middle of a streak of ten straight ATA women's singles championships, and she had become the first black player to compete at both the U.S. National Championships, in 1950, and Wimbledon, in 1951. For reasons I'll explain in depth soon, Wilmington had become her second home, and she played every day on the Orange Street court. Althea's words that day to me, a little five-year-old boy who had never picked up a tennis racket, gave shape to my dream and still bring me to tears every time I remember them.

Mr. Jackson said to her, "Althea, I want you to meet my good friend Lendward Simpson, my next-door neighbor." And she looked down at me and said, "Lendward, it's nice to meet you. But what took you so long, champ?" It still takes my breath away to think about the inspiration of her words to me that day and the power they had on a five-year-old knucklehead kid. She spoke something into existence, "champ," that I could never have dreamed for myself at that point. And then, in the coming months and years, she backed up those words by becoming one of my first coaches.

Then Althea noticed something: I was finally in the promised land, my eyes as big as dinner plates, but my hands were empty. She said, "Mr. Jackson, does he have a racket to play with?" He said I didn't, so she quickly handed me hers and told me she was giving it to me. That racket instantly became my most treasured possession, of course, even though I didn't understand that it was a gift from one of the most incomparable legends in the history of tennis. I only knew that I might actually get a chance to join in the fun.

But first, I learned what my primary tasks would be when the adults competed in their afternoon matches. Mr. Jackson showed me how to run balls during their games, and then he showed me how to sweep the court between matches. Those were my jobs, and I was so thrilled to be a part of things that it was just icing on the cake when, after they had finished playing, Mr. Jackson and Althea took me over to the backboard and started teaching me the fundamentals of the game. I didn't hit a ball over the net for two whole years; I stood next to those two legends while they coached me in the small things that aren't small at all: skills like the proper swing for a backhand, or the right foot position on a volley.

They would show me a certain swing technique or a step, say, "Now you work on this until we get back," and then they would go sit on the porch overlooking the court, drink their Coca-Colas, and watch me. I could hear them chatting and laughing, probably in part at me because I was so incredibly eager and energetic and I was running around like a whirling dervish. Sometimes they would yell out, "Lendward, you need to be keeping score and let us know what the score is!" Of course, you can't beat the backboard; it returns your hit in the same way every time. So the score was never going to end up in my favor, but I would keep score if they told me to keep score.

But just like I was learning every nuance of each tennis move they taught me, those adults were learning something too as they watched that little boy hustle around the court. They were learning that I was like a brick. I was going to do what they wanted me to do, because I was in the place where I belonged. They had showed me that they cared about me, and I had gotten a taste of the sport I loved, so I was never going to give up. I was thoroughly coachable. I had been ushered in through those mysterious gates, and I was there to stay. Little could I have known what that determination to connect with my neighborhood backyard tennis court would have produced more than fifty years later.

I didn't just learn the building blocks of tennis at 1406 Orange Street during those formative years; I also learned the fundamentals of sportsmanship, hard work, discipline, and so much more. I had a front row seat as Dr. Eaton and his friends, all key professionals in Wilmington's black community, talked about the injustices in their community and strategized ways to fight for equal opportunities. That tennis court was like the war room for a protracted and multifaceted battle that would make Dr. Eaton the leading civil rights warrior in Wilmington, and as I swept the courts and practiced my swing against the backboard I also listened to everything they said, and it shaped me.

My mom, along with Mama Henny, had laid the foundation of my faith and instilled discipline in me at home, but on Orange Street I found another vital classroom. Whether it pertained to tennis, equal rights, or tireless work, I learned the key elements of life because I was able to watch my heroes up close. All five of my pillars taught me that I could take the fundamentals that sparked success on the tennis court and apply them to life. And from the first time I had the opportunity to coach and teach young people myself, I have leaned on those same principles and the same hierarchy of emphasizing fundamentals repeatedly early and refusing to add more complicated concepts until students have thoroughly mastered those fundamentals.

I was no longer in the bushes; I was an accepted member of the tennis community at the Eatons' house. I was perfectly content with my role as a helper there and challenged by the daily lessons I was receiving from Althea and Mr. Jackson. For four years I went there nearly every day, and I didn't wish for anything more. But soon a new set of gates would be opened to me, revealing a vast world of tennis with more intense competition and troubling reminders about the barriers that had been suppressing opportunities for talented players like Mr. Jackson for years. My pillars set me up to win and thrive in the sport I was growing to love, but I would have to push against the forces that wanted to hold me back from tennis success.

—⚊—

In 2019 a CBS crew came to Wilmington to film our One Love students for the documentary "Althea and Arthur."

Althea   Lenny   Syndnew   Pauline
                   Lewellyn   Betz

Young Lenny with tennis greats Althea Gibson, Sydney Llewellyn and Pauline Betz

CHAPTER 5

Dr. Eaton

Hubert Eaton grew up first in Newport News, Va. and later in Winston-Salem, N.C., the son of a doctor who made his earliest medical calls in a horse and buggy. He started playing tennis as a teenager in Winston-Salem and won the first tournament he entered—the 1932 North Carolina Interscholastic Tournament. That tournament connected him to Dr. Charles Furlong, a Smithfield doctor who also became Eaton's coach and created a template for the type of mentoring he himself would do on the tennis court for decades to come. Eaton went on to win the ATA National Junior Championship in 1933, an accomplishment that earned him a four-year tennis scholarship to Johnson C. Smith University in Charlotte.

He was a top student and a star tennis player in college, but still he knew that his chances of being admitted to a medical school in the South were slim. In 1938 he accepted an offer to study medicine at the University of Michigan. He was part of a distinguished group, as fewer than fifty black students attended white medical schools in the U.S. that year.

After completing his medical studies in Ann Arbor and his internship at Kate Bitting Reynolds Hospital in Winston-Salem, Dr. Eaton and his wife Celeste, a native of Wilmington, moved back to Celeste's hometown so that Hubert could open his practice. They lived with Celeste's parents for two years until they could buy their own house, and Dr. Eaton selected a home on Orange Street with enough space for a tennis court. The property was on the edge of Wilmington's black neighborhood, but several white families also lived on the block so the real estate agent would only sell him the house through a dummy intermediary owner.

No sooner had the Eatons closed on their home in 1945 then Dr. Eaton called a New York City-based company called Tennis Courts, Inc. This was clearly a priority for Dr. Eaton; he had been in Wilmington long enough to know that the only tennis facilities that allowed black players were subpar, to say the least. He made arrangements for the company to send someone down to Wilmington to build the court, and as he says in his biography, "Shortly thereafter, I went to the bus station to meet John Murray, a middle-aged Scotsman with a well-worn duffle bag. At my home, he took a quick walk over the plot I had selected for the court, took his transit from his bag, and made a few sightings. Puffing on his pipe, he said, 'Doctor, if you can have sufficient clay and cinders hauled in and provide me with four common laborers, I will have you a tennis court here in one week.'"

Dr. Eaton supplied the materials and the workers, and Mr. Murray was true to his word. Less than a week later the court was finished and Dr. Eaton and Nat Jackson were out there hitting, bringing all of their ATA national champion power to bear on that backyard court. I wasn't quite yet a glimmer in my parents' eyes, but the private tennis complex that would play such an instrumental role in my childhood quickly became a fixture among Wilmington's black professional class. He also left a large plot of his land, behind the tennis complex, undeveloped so that neighborhood kids like me could use it as a park, giving us a safe place to play in a city where black children were repeatedly instructed to avoid certain streets and neighborhoods.

Dr. Eaton was committed to his family, his medical practice, and the teaching and promotion of the sport he loved. But as much energy as he devoted to those three pursuits, he still found the drive to battle tirelessly for racial equality. It didn't take long for him to become one of the most prominent civil rights leaders in Wilmington, fighting for everything from equal funding for public schools to the right for black physicians to practice in white hospitals. He wrote his own important chapter in the tumultuous racial history of my hometown, which was bruised by entrenched prejudiced attitudes and practices that severely limited opportunities for black residents. Once North Carolina's largest city because of its busy and prosperous port, Wilmington saw the formation of a powerful and educated black middle class after the Civil War, but a group of white supremacists, threatened by the influence of their black neighbors, organized a tragically historic coup in 1898 that led to the murder of dozens of black people in Wilmington and the dismantling of every black power structure.

I was born just fifty years after the Wilmington race massacre, and the city was still reeling from the effects of so much hate and discord, especially in light of the Jim Crow laws and segregationist attitudes that still dominated the city. Black people could work in blue-collar jobs like restaurants, the shipyard or the railroad, but higher-paying jobs were hard to come by when my parents were starting their family and trying to create stability for my sister Helenda and me. Dr. Eaton was a respected doctor, but when he started practicing in the early '40s he was still restricted to the blacks-only hospital. Everything he did, as a doctor and as a community leader, was designed to expand the opportunities for his black neighbors. The changes Dr. Eaton successfully fought for in our community included:

- Access for black doctors to practice at public hospitals and the integration of those hospitals for patients of any skin color.

- Equal funding for black schools in New Hanover County, and eventually the integration of the public schools. He ran for the school board three times, becoming the first African-American to run for public office in the county since the 1890s.

- The desegregation of Wilmington College, which later became UNC-Wilmington. He was also the first black member and the first black chairman of the UNCW Board of Trustees.

- The integration of the New Hanover County YMCA, the county public library system and the Wilmington Municipal Golf Course.

The most famous recipient of Dr. Eaton's generosity, of course, was Althea Gibson, the original owner of my first tennis racket. As he tells the story in his own biography, Dr. Eaton first saw Althea play in 1946 at the ATA National Championship at Wilberforce University in Ohio. They already knew all about Althea's talent; she had won the ATA national titles the two previous years while still in her teens. As he watched Althea dominate another opponent that day, Dr. Eaton was sitting with Dr. Walter Johnson, and both men were impressed by Althea's presence and movement on the court. Althea was nineteen years old, but when Dr. Eaton and Dr. Johnson did a little research they learned that her childhood in Harlem had been difficult, marked by poverty and instability, and her school attendance had been spotty. They saw tremendous potential for her in tennis but understood that her path would already be difficult enough without being hindered by a lack of education.

Before Althea had finished her match that day, the two doctors had concocted a plan: Dr. Eaton would invite her to come live with his family and train with him in Wilmington, and Dr. Johnson would handle her summer training and pay her expenses on the tournament circuit. As Dr. Eaton recalled, when they called Althea over after she had finished playing he said something to her along the lines of, "You have a very bright future if you are willing to work hard." She heard about the plan and immediately agreed that she would be crazy to pass up such an opportunity.

As Dr. Eaton recalled, he did neglect to think of one significant detail regarding the proposal to relocate Althea—he invited her to move into his home without informing his wife Celeste. "I found myself in a dilemma," he wrote. "If I told Celeste before Althea arrived, she might flatly say that Althea could not come. Although I had a joint commitment with Dr. Johnson to Althea, I knew that I needed my wife's consent and cooperation." He decided to broach the subject with Celeste only if Althea's mother gave her blessing for her daughter to move South. A few days after Eaton returned home from Ohio he received a letter from Althea's mother expressing her support and gratitude for his offer, so he brought the situation to his wife, who agreed to welcome Althea into their home.

When Althea showed up in Wilmington on the late morning train in September 1946, she carried two cardboard suitcases fastened with leather belts and, as Dr. Eaton remembered, a saxophone on a strap around her neck—a gift from the famous boxer Sugar Ray Robinson. As Dr. Eaton wrote, "When she told us that she had not slept all night and had not eaten any breakfast, we suggested that she help herself to whatever she wished from the refrigerator. She prepared five scrambled eggs, a dozen slices of bacon, and five pieces of toast. As she consumed this mammoth meal with a huge glass of milk, I suddenly had doubts about my hasty decision to have Althea live with us."

In the years between her arrival and my first meeting with her in 1953, Althea finished high school, even though the principal at Williston High School originally put her in the freshman class because she had missed so many days of school in New York. She became a conscientious student and got her diploma with the help of the Eatons and a number of their friends in Wilmington. One of her academic tutors, a local educator and civil rights crusader in her own right named Bertha Todd, was a longtime friend of my mom's as well, and she loved to tell stories about the time she spent teaching the young tennis champion. Althea also blazed a brilliant trail through the tennis world in that period, winning ten straight ATA titles from 1947 to 1956 and becoming a pioneer as the first black player to compete at both the U.S. National Championships in 1950 and Wimbledon in 1951.

How do you measure the impact of one spontaneous, generous decision? Dr. Eaton drilled Althea in the fundamentals of tennis, to be sure, but he also taught her about sportsmanship, self-discipline, strategy, and mental toughness. Althea had already demonstrated her talent by the time she moved to Wilmington, but with no more than a ninth grade education and a lack of adult supervision in her younger years, she was hardly poised to be the most legendary trailblazer in the history of tennis. Dr. Eaton was the catalyst in the development of the young player that has inspired, and will continue to inspire, young athletes who think they're facing something insurmountable.

Of course, Dr. Eaton helped change everything for me, too, by welcoming me into the world that he and that efficient Scotsman had created years before I was born. He ushered me into a wonderful world of tennis and stood as a towering example of fighting for justice in your community, standing strong even against intense opposition. Blacks and whites alike fought back against Dr. Eaton's battles for equality in those days; efforts to silence him became so aggressive that he was accused of tax fraud and even indicted on trumped-up murder charges related to the death of a patient. I watched his courage as he fought to clear his name and never wavered in his crusade for justice in education, health care and every other aspect of public life.

As I became older Dr. Eaton used to pull me aside for serious conversations, talks designed to fortify me for the battles he knew I would face along my own road. He was incredibly busy and important and he didn't need to take the time for one young man, but he narrowed his focus so that he could teach me to live with integrity, to be above reproach in all things, and to be authentic and sincere in my dealings with people. As I got out in the world and had my own challenges, I would stop by to ask his advice, and he was unfailingly generous with his advice and his wisdom.

Of course, Celeste was right there alongside him, watching the tennis matches each afternoon and taking a special interest in me when I was just figuring out how to hold my own on a tennis court. When Jo Ann and I had our firstborn daughter in 1979, we named her Celeste in honor of that extraordinary lady.

I always tried to come back to visit Dr. Eaton in his later years, after Celeste had died and he was suffering from Alzheimer's. My appreciation for him has grown as I have come to understand how much responsibility he carried—for the rights of black people in Wilmington, for the black tennis community, and for his patients and family. After he died, an elementary school on Gordon Road in Wilmington was named after him, and a plaque on the house at 1406 Orange Street recognizes his tremendous contributions to his community. He is well-deserving of every honor.

I was privileged to speak at Dr. Eaton's funeral in September 1991, and I was struck by the location of the service: A funeral home on Market Street in Wilmington that had served the white people of the city exclusively for decades. I don't know this for sure, but Dr. Eaton's service might have been the first black funeral that establishment ever hosted. It was so fitting that he would topple one more stronghold of racism even after he was gone.

—⁓—

CHAPTER 6

Safe Haven

From the day I was finally granted entry into Dr. Eaton's tennis facility, I spent as much time there as I possibly could. It was a refuge for me—from my protective parents, from school, and especially from the acute racial tension that we lived in the midst of every day. To grow up in Wilmington in the 1950s was to navigate constant landmines, as we tried to avoid situations and areas of town where we would most certainly face verbal abuse, or worse, because of the color of our skin.

The area where the Eatons, the Jacksons and my family lived was called "The Bottom," because it was the lowest point in a town that already sits just barely above sea level. The Cape Fear River and the downtown business district were a little more than a mile away, but our parents set strict limits on the places we were permitted to explore on our bikes or on foot.

Our house was on Ann Street between 14th and 15th streets, but 15th street was an important boundary for us, because the other side of that street was a white neighborhood. There was actually a white family who lived right across from my family on the corner of 15th and Ann, and while I'm sure I kicked or threw a ball into their yard occasionally I knew better than to try and retrieve it. It was confusing to me as a young boy, and those prohibitions, and the slurs that we heard when we were minding our own business around my hometown, planted seeds of frustration that would make me unwilling to quietly keep to myself as I got older.

The Krispy Kreme donut shop was just three blocks away on Market Street, and those melt-in-your-mouth treats seemed to tempt us all the time when I was a child. Krispy Kreme served us just as it served white patrons, but the route to the store went through a white neighborhood, so each time we walked or rode there we were taking a risk. Every barking dog or stern white face made our hearts beat a bit faster, but the reward was a Krispy Kreme donut! So we kept taking our chances, but it was always a relief when we crossed 14th street and re-entered safe territory, still licking the sugar off our fingers. The Dairy Queen was a frequent destination, because it was the only place we could get ice cream, but if we wanted to eat at the Five and Dime downtown we were prohibited from eating at the big fancy lunch counter. We had to go stand in a tiny corner that was roped off for the black patrons.

The adults in my life wanted to keep me safe, but I still saw some resistance to the status quo that I later adopted in my own attitude. I remember riding with my Aunt Ruth in her car one day when a young white boy hollered racial slurs at us. I'm sure that's the first and last time he ever showed that kind of prejudice and disrespect to my aunt, because buddy, she let him have it. She answered, "What did you say?" and then told him what she thought of his mouth.

When I witness those situations, I internalized the courage displayed by the adults in my life like my mom, Aunt Ruth, and Dr. Eaton. I took it all in; they wanted me to understand that I shouldn't willingly insert myself into dangerous situations, but at the same time I shouldn't be afraid to stand up for myself. They set an example for me and led me to hope that change was possible, even in a deeply divided place like Wilmington with its grim history of racial hate and violence.

The streets around me were fraught with the possibility of conflict, which was one of the chief reasons Dr. Eaton constructed his backyard Eden—so he and his friends could play the sport they loved away from the eyes of prejudice and injustice. I learned how to pass between the different worlds of my hometown and how to fit in and make conversation anywhere. I moved from the street corners in my neighborhood with the tough kids, to the local cab stand where I went with Mr. Jackson to play checkers against the old-timers, to the black professional culture in Dr. Eaton's backyard. That early training meant that I could eventually go from the royal box at Wimbledon, or the president's suite at the U.S. Open to any Southern barbershop or local store.

The Orange Street tennis court, though, became my safe haven. We went around that corner and we were safe. Nobody ever came into Dr. Eaton's world if they weren't invited, and we never heard any ugly remarks back there. We were in our own private and secure world.

Remember, from age five to age eight I never actually hit a tennis ball over the net during my daily visits to Dr. Eaton's yard. I chased after balls, swept the court and practiced fundamentals against the backboard. I was learning, but at that point I was only serving aces and winning points on strategic backhands in my dreams. When I finally had the opportunity to move to the next level in tennis I had one person to thank—Mrs. Celeste Eaton.

Mrs. Eaton liked to sit in the shade on the back porch and watch everything unfold on the court each afternoon, but I was unaware that she had been studying me in particular. She watched me shag balls, sweep the courts and pick up the trash, and she saw me scurry over to the store every day and carry crates of cold Coca-Colas back for the players. She sensed two things: That I would continue to do menial tasks just so I could be near tennis and the great players who congregated there, and that I was ready and willing to learn how to actually play the game. One day she pulled her husband aside, gestured to me and told Dr. Eaton, "I've been watching him, and it's time for him to really start to play this game. Why don't you spend more time with him?"

Now, Dr. Eaton respected his wife's opinions; in his biography he tells a story about how he almost sent Althea Gibson back to New York at Celeste's request when Celeste thought Althea had not supervised the Eaton children closely enough while babysitting. (Althea was only allowed to remain in the home when Celeste relented and gave her a second chance.) He listened that day too, and the next day I rejoiced when Dr. Eaton called me over and told me I would be allowed to start hitting the ball over the net.

Not long after I reached that milestone, Celeste Eaton intervened on my behalf again when she told her husband that she thought I was ready to travel to my first tennis tournament. They decided that the ATA Nationals, which was coming up in Durham, would be a good first competition for me, but when they raised the idea I knew for certain that a major obstacle stood between me and that tournament—my mother. It had taken months and months to convince her to let me walk around the corner! How would she ever agree to let me travel to Durham for a tennis tournament?

Dr. Eaton walked back to my house with me one day to raise the idea with my mother. My mom respected him tremendously, but nonetheless she knew what her answer to his question was and she didn't hesitate to share it. "No. He can't possibly do that. He's way too young." Of course, as soon as Dr.

Eaton walked out the front door I launched into my own lobbying campaign, because I desperately wanted to go on this adventure. Whenever I would ask, my mother would just find new, more emphatic ways to say the word "no."

Finally, though, I begged her so doggedly that my mother came up with a proposal: She would allow me to play in the tournament on the condition that she come along as a chaperone. There were four boys competing in the event— me, Dr. Eaton's son Hubert Jr. and the two brothers who lived next door to the Eatons, Leonard and Thomas Halls. At the age of eight, I was several years younger than the other three, and my mom agreed to come along to act as a guardian for all four of us. I was entered in the singles division and also the doubles division with Leonard Halls, who was eleven.

It was the most exciting thing I had ever experienced in my young life. I still remember the feeling of walking up to the tennis complex in Durham and seeing so many black kids with their rackets, when up to that point I had never even stepped on a tennis court other than the one around the corner. I had no idea what to expect—whether I knew enough to hold my own on those courts or if I was way out of my league—but I was just so thrilled to be there that it really didn't matter. The three older boys from my neighborhood weren't intimidated; they had traveled to tournaments before and they knew what they were doing. So I just followed them and tried to adopt their confident personas.

The first match I played in was in the singles division. Now keep in mind I was one of the youngest boys out there, playing in my first competition. I beat my first opponent and advanced to the next round, and my mom was up there watching me swing a tennis racket for the first time ever, amazed at what she was seeing. But when I lost in the second round, she stopped being a fan and became mom again in a hurry when I refused to shake my opponent's hand. She leapt down from the stands to the court, yanked me by the ear and pulled me over to the net, where I had a sudden and painful change of heart about shaking hands.

Even though I lost my second singles match I was an eight-year-old playing against boys three years my senior, and it was dawning on me that I could really be good at this sport. All of those hours, with Mr. Jackson on one side of me and Althea on the other and only the backboard for an opponent, had yielded actual results that allowed me to outplay older boys in a real tournament. But my biggest triumph of that trip was yet to come.

For the doubles division I was paired with Leonard Halls, a tremendous player whose self-assuredness was contagious. We started winning, defeating pairs who were coming in as the favorites, and before we knew it we had won the whole thing. Here I was, an eight-year-old kid who had not dreamed of such a thing as a youth tennis tournament just six months earlier, and I was holding up a trophy after toppling some of the best young players in the ATA. I was ecstatic! And I couldn't wait to sharpen my skills so that I could win some more.

So many sights and sounds about that day in Durham still linger for me. I had never seen so many tennis courts in one place, and I had never imagined that there were so many other black people who played the game of tennis. It was a wonderful new world. But nothing stands out as distinctly as my mother's reaction when Leonard and I captured the doubles championship. I went up into the stands to find her, and she was crying. She had watched the whole thing unfold, and she cried and cried because she realized that she had done everything in her power to keep me from reaching that point. First when I wanted to go to Dr. Eaton's for the first time when I was five, and again when I asked to play in the tournament, she had resisted until I eventually wore her down.

If I hadn't been such a persistent (some would say pushy) child, we would have missed the chance to experience that victory, and I never would have realized my potential as a tennis player. That day it was like someone flipped a switch in my mother. She didn't stop being protective of me, but her attitude toward my tennis development completely changed. We returned to Wilmington exultant in our victory, and I had trouble thinking of anything but the next opportunity that tennis might bring my way. Like so much of my journey, though, the next door that would open for me was better than I could have imagined.

—⁂—

Dr. Hubert Eaton congratulates me after I won the ATA national boys championship in Wilberforce University in Ohio when I was twelve years old. I received two trophies, for winning both the 12- and 14-year-old titles.

Me, my doubles partner Leonard Halls, Luis Glass, and his brother Sidney Glass at our first-ever ATA tournament in Durham.

CHAPTER 7

The ATA

It's impossible to appreciate my own journey through the tennis world without understanding the history of the American Tennis Association. Founded and sustained by a band of visionaries that includes two of my own pillars, the ATA was unflagging in its support of black players and its commitment to making sure we had opportunities for robust competition. It's an organization that has been absolutely central to my life, yet it is too often underappreciated by sports fans and historians alike.

The ATA is the oldest black sports organization in the nation. It was founded four years earlier than the Negro Baseball League, which has a higher profile, and its impact extended far beyond the promotion of tennis to a broader range of people. As presentations like the "Breaking Barriers" exhibit about the history of black tennis point out, the ATA, in the age of segregation, became a vital source of networking, friendship and educational opportunities for black students and professionals.

The first official black tennis club, the Chautauqua Tennis Club in Philadelphia, was formed less than a decade after the sport was played for the first time on American soil. Tennis is believed to have been played first in this country in the early to mid-1870s, and in 1890 the Chautauqua club was established. In the same year, Booker T. Washington built the first black tennis court at Tuskegee Institute in Alabama.

Black tennis clubs sprung up in Baltimore, Washington DC, and New York City soon after play began at Chautaqua, and the sport spread next to Chicago, where Mary Ann Seames, known to all as "Mother," started teaching tennis to kids on clay or dirt courts as far back as 1906. But until representatives from more than a dozen black tennis clubs organized a Thanksgiving Day meeting in 1916, black tennis lacked any organized structure for competition.

The purpose of that meeting, which was held at the YMCA in Washington DC, was to officially establish the ATA. Shortly after its founding in 1881, the U.S. Lawn Tennis Association had issued a policy statement barring black players from competing in its events, so the growing number of national black tennis enthusiasts resolved to create its own governing body. H. Stanton McCard of Baltimore was elected as the first president of the organization, and other key founders of the ATA were Ralph V. Cook of the Monumental Tennis Club in Baltimore and D.O.W. Holmes of the Association Tennis Club in Washington.

In 1917, the first ATA National Championship was held at Druid Hill Park in Baltimore, with Tally Holmes and Lucy Diggs Slowe making history as the first singles champion. Three decades before my birth, the nationwide network of tennis players and coaches that would provide the framework of my early life had started providing life-changing opportunities for black youth lucky enough to pick up a tennis racket.

The impact of the annual ATA championship tournament grew tremendously in 1925, when the event was hosted on a black college campus for the first time. Attendance at the previous tournaments had been limited by segregation, since potential players and fans had a hard time finding hotel rooms or restaurants that would serve them near the host tennis club. But starting with that 1925 competition played at the Manual Training and Industrial School in Bordentown, N.J., the championships became more accessible for a wide range of black professionals and tennis fans. That year a record-high 5,000 people attended the tournament, and for the next forty-five years nearly every championship was held on a black college campus like Wilberforce University, Tuskegee Institute and Hampton Institute.

As a former ATA player pointed out in a video featured in the Breaking Barriers exhibit, a college campus offered dormitories and dining facilities that were wide open to black attendees, and the annual gathering provided the added benefits of showcasing black college opportunities for the young people who were playing or watching the matches and funneling the money from the event back into those college's coffers. As the ATA's official website explains, "The college administrators were delighted to have so many prosperous and potential donors affiliated with their campuses. The ATA national soon became one of the most anticipated social events of the year in the black community. Formal dances, fashion shows, and other activities were planned during the week of play."

Soon the ATA was sponsoring a full slate of tournaments for juniors and adults at black tennis clubs all over the nation. But even as the ATA grew in popularity and became a top attraction on college campuses across the nation, black tennis leaders like Dr. Eaton and Dr. Johnson were undertaking efforts to integrate the sport. The first inroad to diversifying tennis came in 1940, when legendary white player Don Budge, who had become the first American to win the Grand Slam two years earlier, played in an ATA-sponsored tournament in New York City. Budge competed in both singles and doubles in the event, making a statement about the need for the best tennis players of every color to have access to the top tiers of competition.

Budge's doubles partner at that ATA event had been Dr. Reginald Weir, and in 1948 Dr. Weir crossed the color line himself when he competed in the U.S. Indoor Lawn Tennis Championships in New York. And two years after that, as a result of intense lobbying from Althea Gibson's coaches and mentors Dr. Eaton and Dr. Johnson, USLTA officials finally accepted Althea's application to become the first black competitor at the U.S. National Championships in Forest Hills, N.Y. According to the ATA website, during Althea's first match at Forest Hills a bolt of lightning struck a concrete eagle mounted on the top of the stadium, knocking it to the ground. As she reflected later, "It may have been an omen that things were changing." Althea won her first match that year and lost her second to three-time Wimbledon champion Louise Brough.

The next year, while she was still a student at Florida A&M and showing herself as a force on the ATA stage, Althea became the first black player to compete at Wimbledon, and by 1952 she was ranked seventh in the nation by the USTA. Four years later the benefactor of my first tennis racket was the most dominant tennis player in the world, winning the French Open in 1956, the Australian Open, Wimbledon and the U.S. Open in 1957 and Wimbledon and the U.S. Open again in 1958. Without the determination of the vision of the ATA founders and the personal intervention of Dr. Eaton and Dr. Johnson in her education and training, Althea might never have made it out of the street courts of Harlem to shine on the world's stage.

The intersection of my personal mentors with the ATA started just fifteen years after the organization's founding in 1931, when my future next-door neighbor Nat Jackson won his first doubles championship with his brother Franklyn. Mr. Jackson claimed five more trophies in the 1930s, and then in the next decade Althea Gibson made her entrance into the ATA landscape, winning the girl's championship in 1944 and then, in an extraordinary run, taking every women's singles title from 1947 through 1956.

Through that reign of dominance of the singles division, Althea also teamed up with Dr. R. Walter Johnson, who was such an important mentor and coach for both Althea and me, for a string of mixed doubles triumphs. Althea and Dr. Johnson won the mixed doubles championship every year but one between 1948 and 1955. During that same era Dr. Eaton collected a shelf full of ATA trophies himself, winning men's doubles titles with George Stewart in 1948, 1949, 1951 and 1956.

Less than five years after Althea and Dr. Eaton won their last ATA championships, a young Arthur Ashe took the circuit by storm, competing for the first time in 1960 at the age of seventeen and winning the singles titles for the next three years before moving on to compete with —and defeat— the best players in the world at Grand Slam events and at the Davis Cup. And two years after Arthur played in his last ATA event I played in my first, but I'll tell the details of those tournaments a little later in the book.

Their personal tennis achievements within the ATA were impressive enough, but the most enduring legacy of Dr. Eaton and Dr. Johnson was their commitment to the development of junior players. It's crucial to understand that junior tennis development was a wasteland for talented black youth before these two doctors got involved in the 1950s. Whereas a young white tennis prodigy could choose from dozens of training academies and programs, players like me had only one option—the ATA Junior Development Program founded in 1951 and overseen by Dr. Johnson in his backyard in Lynchburg, Va.

Dr. Johnson invited up to a dozen young players to join him in Lynchburg each summer for an intense regimen of training and competition. Although the purpose of the program was to identify and cultivate promising young black players, he kept his training camp open to all races, and in 1953 former Wimbledon and U.S. Open champion Bobby Riggs even accepted Johnson's invitation to conduct a clinic on the court in Lynchburg. 1953, the year I discovered tennis, was also a landmark year for Dr. Johnson's program because it was the first year Arthur Ashe participated and the first time his ATA junior team was invited to compete in the USLTA Nationals in Kalamazoo, Mich.

The ATA is still active today, hosting a range of junior and adult tournaments that culminate in the national championship each August, and the organization still puts energy and funds into providing opportunities for young black tennis prospects. Through a variety of programs designed to provide coaching, education and financial support to young athletes, the ATA is still living into the mission that Dr. Eaton and Dr. Johnson so perfectly embodied when I was one of those young players desperate for guidance, as stated on its website: "To harness the power of tennis to promote the education, health, and wellness of underserved youth to create the next generation of tennis heroes and community leaders."

—m—

CHAPTER 8
Lynchburg Summers

By the time I competed in that first tournament, Dr. R. Walter Johnson had already been hosting young tennis players at his backyard training center for five years. Aware that talented young black athletes didn't have any options for intensive development, Dr. Johnson took matters into his own hands, and with the help of other tennis advocates like Dr. Eaton the Lynchburg courts soon became the temporary home of ten to twelve young players every summer from early May to early September.

With my success at the ATA Junior Nationals and the foundation that had been laid by Althea and Mr. Jackson, I was the ideal candidate for the Lynchburg summer program. But once again, I found myself facing the impossible task of asking my mother to let me follow another tennis dream that would take me, just nine years old, out of her life for four months.

It had been hard enough to get her to relent when I wanted to walk around the corner to Dr. Eaton's court. Once I cleared that hurdle, it seemed like an insurmountable height to climb to convince her that I should be permitted to play in a tournament three hours from home. But this request would seem like absolute madness to her. I don't know many parents today who would agree to send a nine-year-old away for such a long period of time.

But like I mentioned, there were literally no other training opportunities for young black players like me. Promising black athletes might be able to play local matches at an ATA-sponsored tennis club, or a small percentage might have been lucky enough to have a neighbor like Dr. Eaton. But those local options would only advance them so far. For black kids there was only one place to go—a beat-up court in the backyard of a visionary Virginia doctor. If I couldn't convince my mom to let me go, there was a good chance that my dreams of playing big-time tennis would die right there before my ninth birthday.

Starting that fall after my tournament win, we all took turns lobbying my mother in a loop—me, Dr. Eaton, Althea, and Mr. Jackson. As we explained how important the development program was to my growth as a player, and as Dr. Eaton outlined the supervision and safety measures that Dr. Johnson promised for any young person under his care, she eventually again relented. I was so excited when she finally agreed that I could go the following summer, even though there were some strings attached. My mother and father would drive me up there and meet with Dr. Johnson so that they could see the accommodations and he could answer all their questions thoroughly.

I knew I would need to be on my best behavior in Lynchburg, because my mom was so uncertain and nervous about the whole thing. Even though she had witnessed my tennis potential in the stands at that tournament, she still always struggled in retrospect with the decision to let me go to Virginia. As my sister Helenda got older my mom never let her pursue sports, because she felt like she had lost me to tennis. The truth was, I was a little scared myself; I was so young, and as I sat in the backseat for that five-hour drive I felt like I was going to another world. But I loved tennis and I had been told this was the place I needed to go to become a great player.

We pulled up in front of a big three-story house with a big backyard featuring a tennis court. I felt right at home, because this set-up was so similar to the one that had become my second home back in Wilmington. Wide-eyed, I followed my parents inside and met Dr. Johnson, who would become my coach, my schedule manager, and my drill sergeant for the next ten summers. We sat down so he could fill my parents in on the daily schedules and practices of life in his junior tennis kingdom.

Let me be clear: This wasn't a summer camp with a little bit of tennis thrown in for fun. Dr. Johnson ran a strict, intense program built on the following priorities: Tennis, tennis, and more tennis. We woke up thinking about the sport, trained all day and went to bed with thoughts about our strokes and strategies dominating our dreams. Our only scheduled activities that didn't involve tennis focused on yardwork and chores on Dr. Johnson's property. Every day we were assigned a task like mowing, edging, weeding his many flower beds, cleaning out the dog pen, or picking the apples, grapes, and cherries that he grew. We were happy kids when it rained, because we could hang out in Dr. Johnson's big basement and play cards or watch television, but those little breaks were rare. We were expected to show up to the court on time ready to play, work hard through every drill and match and follow Dr. Johnson's rules to the letter. He made it clear from the beginning that if we couldn't abide by his policies we would be sent home.

Dr. Johnson was one tough hombre. I admired him and feared him equally, because I understood pretty quickly that he didn't entertain the notion of gray areas. Something was either right or wrong, and if you were part of his tennis program you were expected to do the right thing every time. He and my mother never really got along, butting heads from that first meeting until I stopped training in Lynchburg a decade later, and I think it was because they were cut from the same cloth—principled and unyielding to a fault.

The junior development program, as conceived and executed by Dr. Johnson, was powered by discipline. He didn't try to endear himself to us as our friend. We knew he cared about us, but he showed us that by pushing us harder every day. Dr. Johnson wasn't into positive reinforcement or warm fuzzies, but we saw his commitment to us in the time he spent and the way he transformed his own home into a tennis academy with one objective: To help us fulfill our dreams.

When my parents finally had all of their questions answered and I was moved into my room in Dr. Johnson's big house, they headed back south to North Carolina and I settled into my new regimen. The younger boys and the girls stayed in the house, but some of the older boys lodged in Dr. Johnson's medical office across town. We all ate our meals around the big table in the dining room, and Mrs. Creasy, one of his nurses who was doing double duty as the cook, prepared all of the food. The spreads we saw before us, especially at dinner, were mind-boggling. Mrs. Creasy regularly prepared the following for dinner: Steaks, lamb chops, beef, ham, chicken, turkey, potatoes, assorted yellow and green vegetables, green salad, milk, custard, soup, and ice cream. I don't mean that we had one of those types of meat each night; we had two or three them every night. Needless to say, nobody ever went hungry.

We were all expected to be on the court ready to play at 6 a.m., whether we were staying in the house or in the office, and I remember mornings in later summers when I had moved to the office and we had to run across Lynchburg before the sun rose so we wouldn't be late to practice. Dr. Johnson's training regimen, which he wrote down in detail, included the following exercises every day: twenty-five push-ups, fifty knee chest jumps, a hundred side straddle hops, various weightlifting reps, and three variations of sprint drills.

One of the most significant moments of my first day in Dr. Johnson's summer program came when he introduced me to my assigned older "buddy"—a fourteen-year-old named Arthur Ashe. I didn't know anything about Arthur as a tennis player yet, although I would soon want to emulate him on the court. But that day he was kind to me as he showed me around and explained the schedule and the rules. In that instant, I found myself with a big brother for the first time. He was tasked with keeping me in line and helping me out when I needed it, and his presence comforted me when I hit a major bout of homesickness in those early days.

As much as I had wanted the chance to go to Lynchburg, I missed home so badly at the beginning of that first summer that Dr. Johnson eventually called my parents and asked them to come up to see me. At that point my mother's desire to have me home was overruled by her determination to teach me to fulfill a commitment. I'm sure she was tempted to just pull me out, but she and my father both knew that the best thing was for me to stay the course. They stayed about three days, giving me a reminder of home, but they emphasized that it was only a visit and I needed to stay where I was. After they went back to North Carolina that time my homesickness had evaporated, and I never pined for home again during a summer in Lynchburg.

When I look back on those summers, I'm amazed at the way Dr. Johnson kept preteen and teenage kids in line, especially when there were plenty of temptations around that could have led us astray. One example was the fully stocked bar in the Johnsons' basement, a room where we hung out on rainy days or in our rare blocks of free time. We were in that basement alone frequently, but not once did I see one of the tennis players consider raiding that liquor stash. We had the proper fear of Dr. Johnson instilled in us, and we knew what the consequences would have been if we had stepped over that line.

One of the most talented players in our program was Horace "Red" Cunningham; he beat Arthur Ashe every time he played him, but he also thought he was above Dr. Johnson's rules because he was a local boy who lived right across the street. One morning we were preparing to leave for a tournament in New Haven, Conn., and we were out packing the car at 2 a.m. (We always left long before the crack of dawn because we wouldn't be able to find a hotel that would allow us to stay overnight on our road trips.)

On this particular early morning, I was out helping load our gear when I thought I saw something moving in Dr. Johnson's rose garden. I went over to investigate and discovered Red, working hard pulling weeds. He had run his mouth one too many times, calling Dr. Johnson a turkey, and Dr. Johnson told him that he would have to stay home from the weekend tournament unless he weeded the whole bed by himself. Dr. Johnson inspected his work, and he grabbed his bag and made the trip with us, a little quieter and a little humbler.

The only rebellious act I remember most of us risking had to do with junk food. Dr. Johnson's rules around our diet were as strict as everything else in Lynchburg; we were not permitted to drink soda or eat candy, chips, or any other non-nutritious snacks. But there was a convenience store located right across the street from his house, and sometimes the temptation was just too much for us to bear. We would dash over and get a Coke like we were on an undercover spy operation and drink it as fast as we could. If we heard Dr. Johnson's car coming into the driveway, we would throw the bottle up into the branch of a nearby tree. I'm sure there were times when a brisk wind dislodged dozens of wrappers and bottles and exposed our indiscretions, but at the time we thought we were being clever.

Dr. Johnson certainly looked the other way a time or two when he suspected we were sneaking pop or candy, but he steadfastly demanded that we respect him and each other. I was a notoriously hardheaded child, and once I moved past my brief homesick phase during that first summer I started to get a little big for my britches. My attitude flared one day in a most unfortunate incident that almost ended my tennis career before it started.

Dr. Johnson created a schedule each day detailing who would use the court at certain times, and he put an eighteen-year-old girl named Bessie in charge of enforcing the schedule. That day, after I had been in Lynchburg about a month, my doubles partner Lewis Glass and I practiced and started playing a match, but our time ran out before we finished the match. Bessie came out and said, "You have to give the court up now," and I started to argue with her. Neither one of us wanted to quit, but Lewis was smart enough to keep his mouth shut and let me, always the smart aleck, get in trouble. Before I knew it I let my frustration boil over and I exploded at Bessie: "You black, ugly thing."

Back in those days, calling someone "black" was the worst slur there was, so I expected Bessie to tell Dr. Johnson what had happened. That night at dinner I was terrified of what might happen, but we had a normal dinner, with everyone talking about their day, and when we were finished we split up into assigned groups to clean up the kitchen. I was thinking, "This is unbelievable. I think I might actually get away it," when I heard Dr. Johnson call out, "Lendward, I want to see you."

I walked to the back of the kitchen where Dr. Johnson was sitting with dread sitting heavy in my stomach. He let me have it, telling me that I should never call anyone that name, that I should be ashamed for treating Bessie with such disrespect. I was crying my eyes out, but even through my regret I was thinking that this tongue lashing was my whole punishment, and it wasn't too bad. Once he was done with his lecture, I thought it was over. I couldn't have been more wrong. Suddenly he said, "Now I need you to go upstairs and pack your bags. You're going home." He called Arthur over and told him to go upstairs and help me pack.

I was devastated. I couldn't believe I had ruined this opportunity, that I would have to go back to Wilmington and face my parents and everyone at Dr. Eaton's house who had helped me get to that point. Arthur didn't say much of anything to me as he helped me put my clothes in my suitcase, and I tossed and turned that night, wishing I could get that moment back and control my mouth.

The next morning Dr. Johnson drove me to the bus station, gave the driver extra money to look after me, and put me on the bus by myself for the seven-hour trip back to Wilmington. I'm sure that was the saddest, loneliest seven hours a boy ever spent. Dr. Johnson had, of course, called my parents to tell them what had happened and to alert them of my arrival time, so they were waiting at the bus station for me. I walked down those bus stairs ashamed and embarrassed, and my parents didn't waste any time letting me know how disappointed they were.

I resolved to stay far away from the Eatons' house, because I couldn't face them, or Althea or Mr. Jackson. Fortunately, I didn't have long to hide in my house, because what I didn't know was that Dr. Johnson had prearranged a plan with my parents. I would take that long, forlorn bus ride home, but after just one day they would drive me back to Lynchburg. You have never seen a boy more grateful for a second chance! After I moved back into my room on the top floor of Dr. Johnson's house, suffice it to say my attitude had been transformed.

Dr. Eaton and Dr. Johnson were men of steel. They never coddled us, because they felt they had a responsibility to prepare us for the opposition that was coming. They wanted us to improve on the tennis court, but far more importantly they wanted us to make the right choices in life so that we would keep doing the right thing when we faced truly difficult circumstances as black tennis players in the fractured American South.

—᙭—

I spent hours every day working on tennis fundamentals at Dr. Johnson's summer program.

I prepare to serve at a summer tournament

CHAPTER 9
Dr. J

Unlike me and the other young people who moved into his home every summer for twenty years, R. Walter Johnson didn't grow up on a tennis court. The training ground for Dr. Johnson's toughness, discipline and competitive spirit was a football field, and if college and professional football had been integrated when he was a young man I might never have met him, because he would have found fame on the gridiron.

As the quarterback for Lincoln University in Pennsylvania in the early '20s Johnson was completely unstoppable, once scoring eight touchdowns in a single game and earning the nickname "Whirlwind" for his extraordinary speed between the endzones. When he graduated in 1924 he wasn't ready to leave football behind, so he coached high school teams for four years in Virginia and Texas before putting the whistle down and chasing another dream by enrolling at Meharry Medical College in Nashville, Tenn. Founded in 1876, Meharry was the first medical school for black people in the South, and its notable alumni include, in addition to Johnson, Dr. Edward Cooper, the first black president of the American Heart Association, and Theresa Greene Reid, the nation's first black woman epidemiologist.

After finishing his studies at Meharry, Dr. Johnson went to Prairie View Hospital in Texas for his internship, and it was there that he picked up his first tennis racket. He immediately fell in love with the sport, and in keeping with his driven personality he committed himself to learning everything he could about tennis, even as he opened his own medical practice in Lynchburg. Like Dr. Eaton, he built a tennis court on his property, and he started inviting young talented players like Mr. Jackson to train with him in the 1930s.

He became a formidable player, especially when paired with Althea in the mixed double division of the ATA circuit. The pair won seven mixed doubles titles in eight years in the late '40s and early '50s, which is even more incredible when you consider that Dr. Johnson was nearly fifty years old when they started competing together. But even as Dr. Johnson was winning his own titles as a tennis player, his true focus was always on the development of young players like Althea, Arthur, me, and nearly two hundred others.

After the two doctors watched Althea compete that day in Ohio and resolved to partner to fortify her training and education, Althea made her move to Wilmington and started traveling to ATA events with Dr. Johnson in the summers, before he had officially established the junior program. In her biography, Althea remembered her first summer traveling the Eastern U.S. with Dr. Johnson and other players he had recruited.

"Along about the first of July, we would start to travel," she recalled. "Dr. Johnson had a big Buick and he packed six or seven of us in it, with our bags stuffed in the trunk and a big luggage rack bolted on the roof. We played in Washington, Philadelphia, New York, and New Jersey, and then we all jammed in the car and headed for Kentucky. Dr. Johnson wanted us to play in a little tournament there; I think a friend of his was the manager. But the doctor had the good sense to fly ahead and let the rest of us come on in the Buick."

My own memories, a decade after Althea's, aren't all that different from hers. Dr. Johnson bought a new Buick Roadmaster every two years; he had to, because he wore his cars out driving carloads of young athletes to tournaments in cities like Louisville, Philadelphia, New York, and Washington DC. We would have three people in the front seat counting Dr. Johnson behind the wheel, and four in the back, but often the older players from our program were playing in a different location, conveyed to their tournament by bus or train. Because the events were often divided by age groups, Dr. Johnson couldn't be with all his young players at the same time, so he arranged the transportation for the older players and took them to the bus or train himself. I remember the first time he put me on the train in Lynchburg at eleven years old to travel to a tournament alone; he put cash in my suitcase and instructed me never to take it out en route, and he paid the conductor to look after me. I would be met at the station in New Jersey by Miss Creasy's sister, whose house I would stay in during my tournament. He pledged to parents that he would take care of their sons and daughters, so I'm sure the logistics of getting children to multiple tournaments was overwhelming, especially in the age of Jim Crow.

Fifty years before a movie was made about it, Dr. Johnson introduced us to the real-life Green Book, which was invaluable for him as he found restaurants and boarding houses for us on the ATA circuit. We never attempted to eat at a white restaurant, but instead we consulted the Green Book to find an establishment run by black people. In the North we were usually able to stay at a local YMCA, but in the South we relied on the hospitality of Dr. Johnson's friends who would put us up in their spare rooms. Dr. Johnson had been cultivating those relationships for years, creating a huge network that had been passed on to him from generation to generation. The Green Book represented a wealth of knowledge not just about where *to* go, but also where *not* to go.

It's important to understand that if you were a black person traveling in the South during the Jim Crow era, you had nowhere to stay, nowhere to eat, nowhere to go to the bathroom unless you were sure that place was safe. It was a major problem when you were on a road trip, it was three or four in the morning, and you didn't have a place to relieve yourself. We would find the closest tree, go as fast as we could and jump back in the car. I honestly don't know what the girls did. I've had people ask me whether I felt pressure when I playing in major tournaments or when I was facing a particularly strong opponent, and I always answer them: "We never felt pressure. You know why? Because when it's three in the morning and you have nowhere to go to the bathroom and you have to hold it, *that's* pressure."

Dr. Johnson wanted us to learn discipline and improve our tennis game, but his number one priority was to keep us safe. He promised our moms and dads he would protect us no matter what, and especially when we were on the road in the segregated South there were plenty of risks. If we went to a movie, sitting in the colored balcony with one small popcorn machine and a tiny candy selection, he would go with us to make sure everything went smoothly. We never got invited to a single party or social event that the tournament organizers hosted, not once. We all went through so much just to have the opportunity hit a tennis ball. Our white opponents had a smooth and easy road to those tournaments, but ours was anything but smooth. We were hitting the same tennis ball, but everything else about our experience was completely different.

The first major triumph for Drs. Eaton and Johnson came at the 1950 ATA Championships at Wilberforce University, when the ATA secretary Bertram Baker announced that Althea had been permitted to play in the USLTA national championships that would be held at Forest Hills later that summer. Baker, who had fought tirelessly with Dr. Eaton and Dr. Johnson for Althea's inclusion, referred to those efforts when he said, "Many of us have worked untiringly for years to witness the day when our players would be accepted for competition in the National Championships of the USLTA. That day has come. It was not brought about by senseless agitation or unwarranted demands, but by the cultivation of good will thereby acquiring the genuine friendship of individuals without whose aid the door would not yet have been opened to us."

The year after he sat in the stands at Forest Hills and watched Althea's historic achievement, Dr. Johnson officially formed his Junior Development Program. In Althea, he had a glimpse of what could be possible if the road he had helped pave for her could be scaled for scores of young people he hadn't met yet. And two years after Dr. Johnson welcomed his first junior players in 1951, a ten-year-old Richmond boy named Arthur Ashe moved into the big brick house for his first summer under Dr. Johnson's tutelage.

According to the Whirlwind Foundation, which exists to preserve Dr. Johnson's legacy and raise funds for the restoration of his home and tennis court in Lynchburg, he invited 200 young players to his program over two decades starting in 1951, and yet he still found time to take care of patients at his busy practice and crusade for civil rights breakthroughs in Lynchburg. In a parallel milestone to his friend Dr. Hubert Eaton in Wilmington, Dr. Johnson was the first black doctor to be granted practice rights at Lynchburg General Hospital, and he was also the first black physician to deliver a baby in that facility.

I was too young to really grasp what Dr. Johnson's commitment to his junior players would require during those four months when the training program was operating each summer. He had a little bit of help, like his nurse who cooked for us every day, but for the most part he managed the practice schedules, the logistics of our food and lodging, and the transportation and registration for our tournaments by himself. He paid for our travel and our considerable expenses out of his own pocket. He was strict with us, but his unyielding commitment to helping us become better athletes and people shined through in the way he gave of himself through those summers of training and competition.

"Dr. J, as his players called him, was more than a coach," the website whirlwindjohnson.org said. "He was a teacher and a role model. He was a talent scout par excellence who could spot and develop untapped potential. He preached perseverance, patience, sportsmanship, etiquette, humility and hard work."

When he sent me home for disrespecting the older player he had put in authority over me, Dr. Johnson showed me that he cared about far more than my tennis skills. He modeled the character qualities that he knew would guide me through life, and as time went on I wanted nothing more than to make him proud of me. We might not have understood it fully when we were younger, but Dr. Johnson was infusing us with courage and integrity so that we could withstand the prejudices that lay ahead and continue to blaze a trail through the mostly white world of tennis.

His philosophy of playing the game was all about honesty and integrity. He instructed us to play the balls that were an inch or two out of bounds, because then, when we won against white opponents, no one could accuse us of cheating or seeking any type of advantage. If one of our balls was called out but it was obviously in, we could only say, "Are you sure?" And we could only accept the call that they made—no arguments. (I actually think it made us better players, because our court was essentially smaller than our opponents' court.) It wasn't enough for us to follow the rules, we had to be above reproach in every way. He coached us not to show emotions— negative or positive—so as not to draw too much attention to ourselves on the court. Years later, when Arthur Ashe won the U.S. Open, he showed emotion for the first time, and it seemed strange to me because I realized I had never seen him do that before. He had every right to celebrate, but it didn't come naturally to him because he had been trained by Dr. Johnson to keep all of his emotions under the surface.

We had to work three times as hard as our white opponents, and while we didn't think that was fair, we listened to Dr. Johnson because we knew he saw the bigger picture of what we were trying to accomplish. And since we worked so much harder and adhered to the rules so much more closely than the white players, we discovered that we were stronger and more fit than they were. It came from chasing down so many balls that were actually out of bounds.

My good friend Leslie Allen, who trained with Dr. Johnson in the '60s and went on to achieve a top twenty WTA ranking in 1983, told the New York Times that she wasn't even enthusiastic about tennis during her two summers in Lynchburg, but she knows now that Dr. Johnson's court was at training ground for so much more. "I grew up in a time in the '60s when as a person of color and female, you were told you had to be twice as good in order to be accepted," she said in a 2017 article about the renovation of the court. "You had to work twice as hard in order to be accepted in whatever you wanted to do, whatever career it would be. This fell right in line. Essentially, as I look back on Dr. Johnson, he was preparing us for a world that didn't want us. If we could survive what he threw at us, we could survive anywhere."

In 2017 Dr. Johnson's grandson Lange Johnson told The Amsterdam News of his own experience traveling to tournaments during those summers, and he emphasized that the tremendous investment he made in setting up a top-notch tennis experience for his charges wasn't only for the sake of integrating the sport. Dr. Johnson wanted to make an impression of excellence on the tennis community. "He wanted to win, which was how he believed he could make sure change would last," said Lange Johnson, who died of ALS in 2022.

As tennis greats like John McEnroe and former USTA chairman Alan Schwartz have said, the international success that Althea and Arthur achieved would not have been possible without Dr. Johnson's role in their development. Even though he is known as "the godfather of black tennis," in some ways Dr. Johnson is one of the forgotten giants of American tennis history, but a documentary about his life and a campaign to fully restore his home and tennis court were both ongoing in 2022. I was blessed to be in Lynchburg in May 2018 for the dedication of the restored court, which is the first step in a multiphase plan that will include landscaping, a new monument to Dr. Johnson's work and the renovation of his home into a museum honoring the champions who were trained on that property.

When Dr. Johnson died on June 28, 1971 the New York Times ran an article about his impact on the sport of tennis, but his induction into the Virginia Sports Hall of Fame (1972), the Mid-Atlantic Tennis Hall of Fame (1988) and the International Tennis Hall of Fame (2009) would unfortunately come after his death. At the International Tennis Hall of Fame induction Dr.

Johnson's grandson accepted the honor in memory of Dr. Johnson and spoke of the enduring power of his grandfather's steadfast principles.

"It can be done, no matter the obstacle," Lange Johnson said. "Seeing great raw talent and forming them into great tennis players? It can be done. No integration in the top ranks of tennis? It can be done. No state-of-the-art facility and equipment for African-American players? It can be done."

—ɯ—

Dr. Johnson was an important mentor and teacher for Althea Gibson.

CHAPTER 10

On the Road

The ATA owes its vitality in the twentieth century to Dr. Eaton and Dr. Johnson. During the decade when I was spending my summers traveling the country playing the ATA circuit, and for some years before and after my involvement, these two men were identifying, coaching and funding junior players from all over and also working to keep top black tennis players in the national spotlight.

No one will ever know how much money the two tennis-loving doctors spent out of their pockets to support young players like me. Dr. Johnson even gave us his time and money over our Christmas breaks, when he would drive me and Luis Glass halfway across the country to St. Louis each December to train with Richard Hudlin, a black tennis coach there who also worked with both Althea and Arthur.

Dr. Eaton laid the foundation and Dr. Johnson carried me through every summer to expand my game and my world, and then they both helped pave the way for an educational opportunity that would further change my life. I was too young and naïve to see the big picture, but with his unyielding discipline and his strict standards Dr. Johnson was preparing me and my fellow players for life. Author Eric Allen Hall describes Dr. Johnson's mission well in his book, "Arthur Ashe: Tennis and Justice in the Civil Rights Era."

Hall writes, "More than a tennis camp, Johnson's Junior Development Program was a life lesson, offering strategies for survival in a world of tennis alien to blacks and the working class. To succeed in the predominantly white, upper-class world of competitive tennis, his pupils had to be disciplined and tough, knowing when to fight and, more importantly, when to walk away."

Walking away was not an easy concept for me to grasp in those days; it was my stubbornness and smart mouth that almost got me kicked out of Dr. Johnson's program in my very first summer. But after I returned from that brief suspension and slid into the rhythm of early mornings and hours of work out in the hot sun, I began to build physical and emotional muscle. Dr. Johnson knew that if I reacted to that segregated world with hotheaded impulse I would never get anywhere. Near the end of that first summer, I learned that lesson vividly when we drove all the way to Chattanooga, only to get rejected and turned back to Lynchburg.

The occasion was the USLTA Junior Championships, and despite opposition from the all-white USLTA in the past Dr. Johnson was determined to give his players a chance to compete against the best competition of every color. So three of us got into Dr. Johnson's car and traveled sixteen hours to the Manker Patten Tennis Club in Chattanooga. When we arrived at the facility we walked up to the registration desk, but the tournament officials took one look at us and informed us we were not permitted to play. Dr. Johnson had paid our fees and registered us in advance, but they said that we were disqualified from participation because of the policies in place at that private tennis club.

I was absolutely furious. There's no telling what I might have done or said if I had been left to my own devices as a nine-year-old who thought I knew everything. But thankfully, I was learning to look to Dr. Johnson as my example, and that day he was as calm and collected as I ever recall seeing him. It was unbelievable; with his head held high he turned from that table, and quietly told us to follow him back to the car, and then we loaded up and made the long drive home. When we were back on the road, Dr. Johnson let us vent and cry, and when we had let it all out he said words I will never forget. He said, "Don't ever forget this. Use it to your benefit. Learn from this, because you see what I'm trying to prepare you for. There are people in this world who do not want you playing tennis in their tournaments, but this is what you're going to have to go through. Use this moment to your advantage."

When we got back to Virginia, Dr. Johnson promptly filed a complaint with the USLTA, letting them know what had happened and lobbying for a place in the next junior nationals, scheduled for a different tennis club in Chattanooga. The association went to bat for him and told the Signal Mountain Country

Club that the event would be taken away and moved to a northern site if they didn't allow black players to participate.

So the next summer, when I was ten, we made the same trip to Chattanooga, and I'm fairly confident the tournament officials weren't ready for what we hit them with. My doubles partner Luis Glass and I played some of the best tennis of our lives, and we ended up in the national semifinals. No one had seen us play before, so our ascendance was totally unexpected. Then my mixed doubles partner and friend Bonnie Logan dominated the event and ended up winning her division in singles!

We were so proud of our accomplishments, especially after all we had been through the previous year. It was clear that Dr. Johnson was doing more than enough to prepare us for the top levels of competition. But unfortunately, not even that triumph could have a happy ending. Shortly after Bonnie returned home with her championship trophy, the USLTA informed Dr. Johnson that she would have to send it back, that she had been disqualified from the tournament and her victory had been nullified because she had "falsified her application."

Now, when Dr. Johnson had registered Bonnie for the event he had told the officials that she would turn eleven in the middle of the tournament. He wanted to fully disclose the fact that her birthday fell during the competition, since that could change her age classification. They told him that it wasn't a problem—until she won the whole thing. Suddenly, they had to come up with a reason to delegitimize her victory, so they literally took a trophy back from a ten-year-old child. It was just unbearable.

Bonnie, who has been a lifelong friend of mine, became a tennis legend; among other accolades she won seven straight ATA singles titles and, in 1971, became the first black woman ever to play on the Virginia Slims Tennis Tour. I know she never forgot the sting of that experience when she lost her trophy, but I know just as certainly that she learned how to respond from the strong, unflappable nature of our mentor Dr. Johnson. The lesson—to keep our head up, learn from the slights and keep working hard to win the next battle—was one I would need reinforced over and over. And the next time I sat in that difficult classroom, my teacher was my "tennis big brother," Arthur Ashe.

I was twelve and Arthur was eighteen in the summer of 1961, and we were competing in the USLTA Junior Championships in Kalamazoo, Mich. If Arthur played well enough at that tournament, he had a chance to make history as the first black player ever to qualify for the U.S. Junior Davis Cup team, and of course we knew he was talented enough to win the USLTA junior title. He defeated his quarterfinal opponent, and we were thrilled because we believed he had done enough for Davis Cup selection. When he went to turn in his match results to the tournament director he was told, "You need to go on back to the dormitory to take a shower, because you're playing your semifinal match in one hour."

We were stunned. It was unheard of for a player to be given such a short turnaround between matches! It was clear to me that the tournament was trying to keep Arthur from advancing any further because he was black. I was fuming as Arthur and I walked as quickly as we could back to his dorm room. While I complained, Arthur was as calm and relaxed as he could be. He turned to me and said, "Let's go Lendward, we've got to go back to the dorm, and I've got to take a shower to get ready for my next match."

When we returned to the building, I hadn't cooled down at all. I asked him, "Aren't you mad? What's wrong with you? Don't you understand what they're doing to you?" He quietly prepared to shower and change, until finally my protestations became too much for him. He turned to me and said, "I want you to sit down. I've got to tell you something. I've got to go get ready to play my next match."

"There's no way you can play this match!" I objected.

"Listen, we've got to understand we're playing for somebody else," he replied. "You're not playing for yourself. You're playing for the future of other players. I'm going upstairs, I want you to think about what I just said. When I come back down, you're either on my side or you're not on my side." Arthur didn't pull out a victory in that rushed semifinal, but he imparted an indelible lesson to me, one that helped me keep my quick tongue in check in the years to come.

That was Arthur's last summer with me in Dr. Johnson's program; soon he would be headed to UCLA, and seven years after that frustrating USLTA event he won his first of three Grand Slam singles titles. It's no exaggeration at all to say that Arthur's dignity, grace, and excellence changed our sport forever, and the seeds of his transformative effect were in full evidence when he was traveling the country with me when he was a teenager.

Early in my teen years, I was playing in an ATA tournament in Washington DC when a stranger, whose identity I have never learned, asked to talk to my coach about an opportunity. This person felt like I would be a good candidate for boarding school, knowing that my educational and athletic future would be better served if I could switch to an academically rigorous school away from the restraints of segregation. After this "angel" talked about my future with Dr. Eaton, they arranged for me to take the entrance exam that would determine my qualifications for the top private schools in the Northeast. My scores on the test were high enough to get me in to any of the top five prep schools in the country, but a little more investigation led me to Hill School, which offered a full academic and athletic scholarship.

Of course, this opportunity commenced another battle with my mother, who had already spent three summers without me and was not at all thrilled at the prospect of parting with me during the school year as well. Dr. Eaton's son Hubert Jr. had gone to boarding school in Massachusetts already, and Dr. Eaton and I both appealed to my mother's deeply held commitment to education as we discussed my future. She knew as well as anybody that my options were limited in New Hanover County public schools, so even though she wasn't ready for me to move away she eventually agreed that the scholarship was too promising to pass up.

Boarding school would be an entirely new world for me. For the first time I would have to figure out how to get along as a minority, and before I was even admitted I had to pass a rigorous entrance examination that signaled one thing clearly—I would be swimming in much deeper academic waters than any I had experienced in grade school in Wilmington. As I traveled and played tennis with Dr. Johnson the summer before I enrolled at The Hill School, I was naturally a little nervous about the new world that lay ahead. But I was well-prepared for the challenges, thanks to these two extraordinary doctors who were helping pave a path for me that I could never have imagined for myself.

—⚹—

As my note on this picture states, I won all of these trophies when I was eleven, from several different states in a variety of tournaments.

Me and Bonnie Logan with our mixed doubles championship trophies at the 1962 ATA National Championship at Wilberforce University in Ohio

Scott, Coneya, Bonnie, Luis, Elmer, me and Mrs. Langhorne at the USLTA Junior Championships in Chattanooga

CHAPTER 11

Prep School

When I moved into my dorm at The Hill School and met my white roommate, I had all the evidence I needed that I had left the segregated South behind. I was one of four black students at a school of 400, and I was the only black player on the tennis, basketball and soccer teams. I'm not naïve enough to think that ugly things weren't said behind my back, of course, but what I found when I arrived at that beautiful campus was a refreshing atmosphere that would give me the same opportunities as my white classmates.

The list of Hill School distinguished alumni reads like a "Who's Who" of every major sector in American society. Former Secretary of State James Baker, author James Michener and actors James Cromwell and Harry Hamlin are just a few of those who attended Hill School, along with a variety of U.S. Representatives, state senators, film producers, scientists, and professional athletes. My doubles partner was none other than legendary film producer Oliver Stone, although I and all his Hill School friends knew him as "Bill," and one of my roommates there went on to become a highly regarded artist. I marvel when I think of my journey there from coastal North Carolina. I wasn't exactly typical upper-echelon prep school material, but like as in so many events in my life, I discovered that God had surprising plans for me.

The more time I spent at Hill School—excelling in the classroom and in sports, being treated as an equal in the school community—the harder it became to visit my hometown. It was the early to mid-'60s, and Wilmington activists like Dr. Hubert Eaton were on the front lines of a contentious battle for civil rights there. The Civil Rights Act had not yet passed in Congress, and separate facilities had been the norm for so long down there that my friends and family had become accustomed to them. But I was living with one foot in each of two distinctly different worlds, so I when I went from North to South I found that I couldn't just concede the status quo.

I was only twelve years old when I came home for my first Christmas break, and shortly after I returned to Wilmington my mom realized that I had a severe cold and I needed to go to the doctor. She liked to take us to the old white doctor in the small town of Burgaw who had treated her and her family members for decades, so she made an appointment with him one Saturday and drove me out to Burgaw.

When we arrived, I discovered that the office had a white waiting room and a colored waiting room, and the fight rose up in me. I had shared every type of facility with white people at school for months, and I found that I was absolutely unwilling to go backwards. I told my mother that even though I was sick, I would wait outside in the bitter December air. She tried everything to get me to come sit inside, but I refused, and soon she realized that I wasn't going to budge so we waited outside together.

Finally we were called back to the exam room, and when my mother greeted the doctor I realized that she, as well as my aunt and other relatives, had been telling him stories about my tennis accomplishments and my enrollment in prep school. He wanted to ask me a bunch of questions about the things I was doing, but I was too mad to engage in small talk with him. I answered the questions I had to answer for the medical exam, and we got out of there as quickly as possible.

I grew to love the community and camaraderie of an all-boys boarding school, and over time I became known for more than my athletic skills. We were permitted to go into town once a week while I was Hill School, and on one of those trips I went into a grocery store and had an epiphany. I saw a loaf of bread and thought of the growing teenage boys on my hall, the boys who were always so hungry after study hall each night. I bought all of the makings for PB and J sandwiches, and that night I started making sandwiches with my door open, well aware that a delicious smell would waft down the hall and lure my friends in. I established a lucrative little startup right out of my room, starting out charging fifty cents a sandwich and soon realizing the demand was so great that I could sell each half for fifty cents and double my profit. Thanks to my brainstorm, spending money was no longer a problem while I was at Hill School.

As I entered my teen years and got more accustomed to the pressures of private school, I continued to work with Dr. Johnson at his summer tennis academy and to win trophies at ATA events. Dr. Johnson moved me up the adult division when I was fourteen, even though I could have played juniors for several more years, because he knew I would only improve if I was faced with more intense competition. Luis Glass and I won our first ATA doubles title in 1964 when I was fifteen, and then we won it again the following year. In mixed doubles Bonnie Logan and I put together an impressive dynasty in the late sixties, winning four straight titles from 1967 to 1970.

I also embraced opportunities to equal the playing field in my favorite sport by playing against white opponents. In 1964 I had a triumph at the same court where Althea had made history fourteen years earlier when I defeated Dick Stockton to capture the singles title at the US Lawn Tennis Association's Eastern Boys 14s Championships at Forest Hills, New York. My success throughout that summer earned me the ultimate prize: An invitation to become the youngest male player ever invited to play in the U.S. National Championships (now the U.S. Open). I held that record until 1987, when Michael Chang, who was also fifteen but a few months younger than I had been, competed in the U.S. Open.

I returned to Forest Hills for the biggest tournament of my life so far, drawing a bye in the first round, and then in the second round, unbelievably, facing my mentor and friend Arthur Ashe. Arthur outscored me and eventually lost in a tight fourth-round match to Australian Anthony Roche, but you will never be able to convince me that it was some kind of a coincidence that, out of 128 players in the field, Arthur and I were matched up so early. That kind of thing happened all the time, a convenient way to thin out the minority players as early as possible. I had the opportunity to play in the U.S. National Championships in 1965 as well, defeating Italian champion Nicola Pietrangeli in the first round and losing to John Reese in the second.

After two years at Hill School, I accepted an athletic and academic scholarship to another one of the nation's top prep schools—Cheshire Academy in Connecticut. Cheshire's reputation and its list of graduates are just as impressive as Hill School's, counting two former Connecticut governors and noted industrialist J.P. Morgan among its alumni. Like I was at the Hill School, I was one of just a handful of black students there, but I decided to move from Hill to Cheshire because Cheshire had a more competitive tennis program and I felt like it was a better fit for me athletically. But I shake my head when I think back to that fall when I entered Cheshire, because no one on campus spoke a word about the fact that I had just come from the U.S. National Championship, where I was the youngest male player ever invited to compete.

You would think that my accomplishment would have been the subject of announcements in school assemblies, articles in alumni publications, or just everyday conversation around campus. But I was totally overlooked. I don't have any doubt that if a white student of my age had played in the nation's most prestigious tournament, the school would have shouted it from the rooftops.

Like Hill School, Cheshire provided an excellent environment for both academics and sports. It was more diverse than Hill School but of course I was still a minority there, and the disorientation I felt from being a black Southerner living primarily in a Northern world continued through my high school years even as the Civil Rights Act finally became law and the unjust separate facilities all over the South started to disappear. I realized that my experiences at prep school and on tennis tours had given me a unique perspective when I came home to Wilmington to visit the summer before my senior year and discovered all my childhood friends up in arms over the closure of Williston School.

Williston had a rich history of academic excellence dating back to Reconstruction, and my friends who had thrived there for years were understandably upset with the local school board's decision to shut its doors and, in response to legislated integration, to send its students to New Hanover High School. But even if I could appreciate their dissatisfaction with being uprooted right before senior year, I had been experiencing outstanding, equitable education alongside white classmates for years and I knew the black youths of Wilmington would be better served if they were no longer segregated.

Advocates of Williston wanted the school board to bring in white students to their campus so the school could stay open, but they lost that battle, creating a simmering tension that resulted in black-led boycott of the schools and subsequent violence and criminal charges for "The Wilmington Ten" in 1971. By that time, my friends and I were in college, but I was witness to the early frustration that led to another terrible chapter in my city's racial history. In 1968, as I listened to my friends and tried to understand their frustration, I knew that

I had been changed for good because I dwelled in both worlds simultaneously.

I resonate with the words of Dr. Eaton, who wrote about the Williston High closing in his own memoir and said that while he understood the black community's emotional investment in the school, he had to focus on the bigger picture. His point of view on the matter reinforces the role his steady activism played in the development of my own opinions about integration, truths that were planted in me before I ever started traveling away from Wilmington regularly. "I was very sympathetic to these sentiments and views, but I felt that it was far more important that we, as blacks, move into the mainstream of American life in all ways and at different levels," he wrote.

In the late '60s, the most contentious debate in the South pertained to school desegregation, but today it's about tearing down statues of leaders who owned slaves or promoted racist policies. Maybe living with one foot in each world for so long helped instruct my opinion on this issue too, but I firmly believe that we need to leave the bad statues standing alongside the good statues. Tearing down the statues won't delete all of the oppression and abuse of black people in this nation, and leaving them up can actually serve as a reminder. When I was a child in North Carolina schools, our state history curriculum failed to tell us the whole story, so I didn't understand the ugly heritage of the things that were done to keep my people down. Now that we talk more freely about that history, the "bad" statues must stay standing to help spark continuing conversations.

As Dr. Eaton and some of my Wilmington friends were on the frontlines of the school battle, I returned to Connecticut for my senior year and one additional preparatory year at Cheshire. I had very little free time, with rigorous study requirements and practice and competition for three different sports teams, but school and tennis stayed at the top of my priority list. I also had to work on campus as a requirement of my scholarship, and it created segregation-like conditions when I and the other black athletes were all required to work in the school's kitchen, supervised by a man who made our lives miserable. Before too long, thankfully, I was pulled off of that work assignment and given the job of sitting at the headmaster's table during meals and saying the prayer before we ate.

Even though I had played against some tough opponents on the summer ATA tour, the level of tennis on the East Coast prep school schedule was considerably more intense, and my hard work through those years yielded the result of making me a much more well-rounded player. While at Cheshire, I won the National Prep Schools Championship in Rye, N.Y. in 1967 and 1968, and I was named a prep school All-American for tennis, basketball and soccer. Like my U.S. Open invitation, my National Prep Schools titles were largely ignored. I remember riding up to New York with my coach Larry Hopkins in his ratty Jeep in the dead of winter to play in the tournament. He made the decision to enter me in the tournament and to accompany me on his own, and when we got back to school with the trophy no one said a word to me about it.

My potential as a goalie on the soccer pitch was so evident to my Cheshire head coach that he lobbied me tirelessly to move to his home country of Germany and train with the national team there. He was convinced that I could become a world-class professional goalie, but despite his repeated appeals, my mother wasn't going to budge. There was simply no way she would give a green light to her son moving to Germany to pursue, of all things, a soccer career.

I have no doubt that the educational and athletic opportunities I embraced at two of the country's top prep schools helped pave my path for college and career, and my association with those two institutions have also made me part of an important lifelong fraternity. Whenever possible, I go back to Hill and Cheshire for class reunions, and last year one of my former classmates from Hill School came by to visit me when he was in Wilmington to compete in a triathlon. I had not seen him since I was fifteen years old, but it seemed like those decades evaporated as we sat in my home and caught up.

Before my friend left that day, he asked me, "What do you need to help with that program you're running for kids here? Then, right on the spot, he wrote out a $10,000 check to support the work we are doing here at One Love Tennis in Wilmington. I was moved to tears, overwhelmed by the brotherhood I had happened upon so many years ago, by God's grace to open that prep school door, and by my gratitude as I look back and see the way that one valuable open door led to the opening of so many others.

—◊—

I shoot a free throw for my team at The Hill School in Pennsylvania.

From left Tony Trabert, me and Dick Savitz before I played in the U.S. Open at age fifteen. Trabert and Savitz were both top Davis Cup players for the U.S.

CHAPTER 12
ETSU

Prep school tennis was highly competitive, so through my years of playing the Cheshire Academy schedule I refined my game and became a legitimate Division I prospect. I loved basketball and was improving in that sport as well, so I was particularly intrigued by schools that could offer me spots on both teams. But before I go into the recruiting journey that led me the right fit, I need to take a quick detour into two college opportunities closer to home that didn't quite become a reality.

When I was a teenager and on a school break, the N.C. State tennis coach, who coached there for more than a decade, came to Wilmington to watch me play. This coach had heard about my success on the ATA and USLTA circuits, as well as my two national prep school titles, and he was prompted to explore the idea of integrating his tennis program in Raleigh. ACC sports had been incredibly slow to bring in black athletes; the first two black basketball players didn't come to N.C. State until 1967. So one year later, this coach was intrigued enough by me to make the trip.

I knew that I could get a top-rate education at NC State and it was only two hours from home, so I was definitely interested, especially if a spot on the basketball team could be part of the offer. After all, every North Carolina boy dreams of competing in the ACC.

But it wasn't to be. Not long after our visit, the coach called me and told me that it wasn't the right time to desegregate the Wolfpack tennis program. As I understood it, he had been subjected to considerable pressure from administrators and donors, so that idea was extinguished before I was ever officially in the recruiting pipeline. Just a few years ago, I was at my N.C. Tennis Hall of Fame induction and I ran into that coach again, long retired and already inducted into the hall of fame himself. He sought me out to tell me that he regretted his failure to push back all those years ago. With the benefit of hindsight, he told me that he wished he had fought for me and for the other black players who could have followed me to N.C. State. He said, "You deserve every bit of this recognition, and I just wanted to apologize."

So it was back to the drawing board for me, as I leaned on the connections of my mentors and my success at one of the top prep schools on the East Coast.Eventually I heard from Coach Larry Castle, the tennis coach at East Tennessee State University in Johnson City, Tenn. Coach Castle was refreshingly nonchalant about the race issue. In fact, he didn't mention the significance of me coming in as the first black tennis player at all, instead selling me on the fact that with me leading the way, they could build up the program and put it on the map. He also sold me with his invitation to suit up for both tennis and basketball (he coached both teams) and his assurance that I would feel at home on the ETSU campus.

I had lived almost exclusively away from the South for the previous five years, so I had some reservations about returning to the land of segregation, but sometimes you just have a feeling something is right. ETSU was offering me academic and athletic scholarships and a chance to play the two sports I loved. I know now that I was choosing to go to the place where I would meet my soulmate—a place that would become a refuge and a home for me in the pivotal years when I were transitioning to adulthood. So I accepted the offer to become a Buccaneer, and in the fall of 1968 I moved into my dorm room on the ETSU campus.

When I arrived at ETSU I was the only black player on the tennis team and on the freshman basketball team, but I was used to that type of situation because of my boarding school experience. And like at Cheshire Academy, my classmates and teammates were welcoming and accepting, an especially surprising reality given the fact that we were in the Deep South. At least in the legal sense, things had changed significantly since the last time I had lived in the South and traveled to tennis tournaments through states like Tennessee, Virginia, and North Carolina. The passage of the Civil Rights Act of 1964 meant that as a college tennis player I could eat at restaurants and stay at hotels with my teammates. The proprietors of those establishments might not have always liked my presence, but they were compelled by the law to serve me.

The ETSU Buccaneers competed in Division I Ohio Valley Conference during that time, and once again I had to rise to the level of more intense competition, and I also carried the burden of leadership as I was named team captain during my freshman year. But tennis and academics weren't my only responsibilities. As I became accustomed to life as a college student, I also started preseason workouts with the basketball team, since I loved both sports and had chosen the university in part because I could play both there. But that experiment only lasted two years, as I soon realized I couldn't keep that many plates spinning and still succeed in the classroom. When I returned to Johnson City as a sophomore, I was only competing in tennis and watching the basketball team as a spectator.

My second opportunity to become an ACC athlete came after I had already been a part of the ETSU team for a couple of years. We played a match against Wake Forest, and afterwards the WFU coach called and raised the prospect of arranging a scholarship for me so that I could transfer to his program. This possibility wasn't something I could immediately dismiss, because WFU was such a highly respected university in a competitive conference, but I was so comfortable with my relationships and my routine at ETSU that it would have been a tough decision for me if it had actually come to fruition. Instead, in a repeat of the N.C. State scenario, that coach came back to me a little while later and told me that the school's leaders weren't quite ready to diversify the tennis program. By then it was 1970! But progress was slow to arrive at some of those Southern universities, especially the private schools that weren't tied to taxpayer money.

The boundaries of the ETSU campus were something like a refuge for me and the other black students. We felt safe on campus, but it seemed like when we stepped outside the campus gates into the town of Johnson City we went back fifty years. To reduce the possibility of tension or conflict when I encountered people in the town, I opted to live on campus for all four years and I tried to be wise when I had some cause to travel around the area. I did need to find a black barbershop to get my hair cut, so I asked around and eventually found a barbershop and also made some friends in Johnson City's black community, and as I got to know more of the faculty at ETSU I found myself adopted by several local families who really enriched my college experience.

There was the Maxey family, who had me over to eat and play badminton regularly. Dr. Maxey, who was one of my professors, was also an outstanding badminton player, and he helped me become so competitive at the game that he entered me in a badminton tournament in Memphis. There were the Webbs, whose two sons became great friends of mine and at whose table I ate many meals. There were the Thorps, and others, and in most cases I became a private tennis instructor for the children in those families and found myself the beneficiary of their frequent hospitality. Through my connections I developed countless lifelong friendships. The ETSU extended family was my family.

Thanks to Coach Castle, I also had a unique and enriching summer job opportunity during my first two years at ETSU. My coach was acquainted with Don Kerbis, who ran the Don Kerbis Tennis Ranch in Watervliet, Michigan. Don Kerbis ran an overnight camp for kids that featured top-notch tennis instruction as well as other activities, like horseback riding. Don recruited all of his tennis coaches from college teams, and he brought together young men and women from all over the world. It was truly a special experience; just a few years after the passage of the Civil Rights Act, Don Kerbis assembled a truly integrated staff. I met a range of new friends at that camp, and we worked together beautifully with no issues. I was just nineteen when I started working there, but not too long ago I received an email from a former Don Kerbis student, reconnecting and telling me about the impact I had on him that summer in Western Michigan.

Through my range of experiences and relationships at that point, I had learned to thrive wherever I was planted, and ETSU was no exception. I was a double major in psychology and physical education, and I found I was well prepared for college academics after the rigors of prep school. I also started collecting wins on the tennis court and made a name for myself in our conference. I played number one in both singles and doubles for all of my four years there, making it to the quarterfinals of the NCAA Tennis Tournament in 1969 at Princeton University and winning the Ohio Valley Conference title in singles four times and in doubles four times.

During the time I was in college, from 1968 to 1972, I also continued to compete on the ATA circuit, returning to Dr. Johnson's court in Lynchburg in the summers to practice and mentor the younger players the way Arthur had guided me. I had my greatest stretch of ATA success during that time in my life, winning four straight mixed doubles championships with Bonnie Logan from 1967 through 1970.

I would always maintain significant connections to Wilmington and Lynchburg because of my relationships with the people in those cities and their importance of my development from a boy into a man, but the ETSU community was special. I was already completely at home there, with countless valuable friendships, when an encounter that started in my psychology class during my sophomore year led to the most meaningful relationship of my life.

—m—

My college tennis team at East Tennessee State University.

OUTSTANDING
COLLEGE ATHLETES
OF AMERICA

This is to certify that

LENDWARD SIMPSON, JR.

has been selected as an Outstanding College Athlete
of America for

1972

In recognition of outstanding ability, accomplishment and service

Henry Kilgore
Henry Kilgore,
Director

Recognition from my successful career at ETSU

In 1974, when I was playing for the Detroit Loves, I visited my old
college team at ETSU.

CHAPTER 13

Jo Ann

I had made lots of friends at East Tennessee State, I liked my professors, and I was winning more often than not on the tennis court. I was halfway through my undergraduate career and I was content in every area except one: I had yet to meet a young lady who really captured my interest. But that changed in the winter quarter of my sophomore year, when a friend in my psychology class decided to introduce me to her friend Jo Ann Buchanan from Erwin, Tenn.

I was taken with Jo Ann right away. She had personality, style, grace, and intelligence. After her friend Patty introduced us I started to run into her on campus frequently, and of course it didn't take me long to ask her out. Jo Ann was a freshman, but she had already become disillusioned with the typical college dating scene, especially when it involved young men in fraternities. She didn't drink and she wasn't interested in frat parties, but when she met me she realized I was different from the norm.

At first glance, it didn't seem like we had anything in common. She had lived all of her life in Erwin, Tenn., a small town about fifteen miles from Johnson City, and she had never been around black people until she came to college. Her family wasn't really into sports, and she knew next to nothing about tennis. But we could sit in the car and talk for hours. Our faith, our values, our ways of looking at the world—they all aligned. "I was just kind of drawn to him," Jo Ann said. "He amazed me. He intrigued me. But I was also always kind of trying to find something wrong with him."

If that sounds harsh, remember that the year we met was 1970 and we were an interracial couple. Even people who were starting to think differently about civil rights, changing their minds slowly as Jim Crow laws had finally gone by the wayside, had a hard time reconciling the idea of black and white people getting married. Like many states, Tennessee still had a law on the books prohibiting interracial marriage, a law that wasn't officially repealed until 1978. But we were able to legally wed in 1973 because of *Loving vs. Virginia,* the 1967 Supreme Court decision that struck down all of the state anti-miscegenation laws.

I present that history for context, but Jo Ann and I weren't researching legal history back in the early seventies when we were getting to know one another. I knew she was the one, but we broke up, by her count, two dozen times because of her trepidation about what our marriage could mean for our families, our safety, our future children, or other scenarios we had not even considered yet. She was afraid, and not without cause. But despite that major roadblock, we kept getting back together. I was a fighter, and I refused to entertain the idea that we might have to live without each other because of the opinions of people who didn't know or understand us.

Even though she grew up in a town with no black residents, Jo Ann had always been sensitive to the racism that was so openly displayed by many people during that era. She has always remembered the day when an administrator at her high school, a man she loved and respected, shouted the "n word" at a sporting event. She wasn't ever able to look him in the eye from that point on. Bands with black members could play at her school, but if opposing basketball teams had black players the crowd turned ugly, and those ugly displays just ate at her. She was unsettled by the hate around her and vividly aware that she viewed the world differently than many of the people in her hometown.

But even though she had those convictions, Jo Ann was gripped with worry about her family in Erwin. She kept our relationship secret from her parents until our engagement, although I had met her younger brother earlier than that when he came to visit ETSU once. Her hometown, like my own, has a difficult racial history, and it was a different era. Eventually, after we were married, the ice around our situation would thaw and her family would invite me into their lives. Over the years I developed good relationships with both her immediate and extended family members, relationships that became closer as we spent time together. But when Jo Ann was still just a college student she was full of apprehension about the effect our decision could have on her parents and her brothers.

I listened to her fears, but I also hung around as closely as I could every time we broke up. She will tell you that I'm notoriously stubborn and I knew what I wanted, and even though the situation was certainly fraught I felt that we had the character and fortitude to withstand whatever was coming. I knew that Jo Ann wouldn't have dated me in the first place if she didn't have that kind of inner strength and an unwavering faith in God's hand in her life.

Jo Ann had to do a bit of spiritual wrestling herself when some family members told her that the Bible prohibited interracial marriage. She and I attended church together every week, and as we explored the scriptures ourselves we confirmed what we already knew: that the Bible says nothing at all about the skin color of the person a Christian chooses to marry. It was still difficult to go against her family's wishes, but Jo Ann was able to move forward with me with the secure knowledge that God had brought us together and He was directing our steps as we planned to spend our lives together.

My family knew about our relationship earlier than Jo Ann's family, but they were contending with their own fears. Jo Ann came home to Wilmington with me a few times while we were dating, and she remembers that my mother was terrified to let us out of the house together. She was absolutely convinced that someone would harm us if they saw us out in public together. During one of Jo Ann's first visits, in early 1971, Wilmington was in the grips of race riots that led to the deaths of two people, several burned businesses and the arrests of a group of protestors known as "The Wilmington Ten." I can't imagine how those incidents stoked my mother's anxiety about our safety on the streets of Wilmington.

It's true that we felt like the ETSU campus was our own secure bubble, but people were worried about us in that community too. Early in our relationship I went to ask Coach Castle for advice about Jo Ann. I think I caught him by surprise when I approached him about it, because even if he had seen us together I don't think he would have brought it up to me. But he did caution me that dating someone of a different race was a serious decision because it could have difficult or even dangerous consequences. He said that I should think about it carefully, but he also said, "If this is what you really want to do, it's fine." Of course, I already knew that dating Jo Ann was what I wanted to do, so I thanked my coach and left the office. He never mentioned it to me again.

But for all of the quiet concern from the adults in our lives, Jo Ann and I experienced almost no outward drama on campus in those early years of our relationship. We got engaged in 1972, which was the year I graduated, and then I started working toward my master's degree in psychology and coaching the Buccaneers tennis team, because by that point Coach Castle had taken a job at Middle Tennessee State. When I fulfilled a lifelong dream of qualifying for Wimbledon that year but was forced to withdraw because of a pulled abdominal muscle, the first person I called from overseas to share my heartbreak was Jo Ann.

We didn't really have to think about where we would get married. We would exchange vows in the chapel on the ETSU campus, in a ceremony officiated by the ETSU campus minister. We could start our life together safe in the community that had brought us together.

We were surrounded by friends, beloved professors, and their families on that happy day—June 1, 1973. But not a single family member attended our wedding. Jo Ann opted to inform her family about our engagement, but we decided it would be best not to invite them. I didn't tell my mother I was married until after the fact, because I knew that even though she and my father would have insisted on coming, she wouldn't be able to let go of her fear that something could happen to us, even on our wedding day. We felt secure on campus, but my mother didn't share our confidence because she didn't know that place and its people like we did. She had heard some terrible things about Tennessee, and as a mother she couldn't get past the fact that her son was marrying a white woman in the South.

Despite all of that it was a beautiful wedding day, the beginning of a marriage that was rooted in love, joy and respect and has proven to be more than strong enough to withstand the storms that have inevitably come our way. That wasn't the end of the story about our relationships with each other's families either; we were committed to patience and prayer as we waited for them to see our devotion to each other and accept our union.

In retrospect, though, perhaps Jo Ann and I became a little too comfortable in our college bubble, a little too sure that if rural Eastern Tennessee could embrace us we would be able to pursue new opportunities without any trouble. Ironically, it was when we left Tennessee for the North that we realized that our bubble had burst and left us vulnerable.

—⁂—

CHAPTER 14
Michigan

Just weeks before Jo Ann and I got married I had graduated from my master's program at ETSU, and throughout that spring of 1973 I had been mining my connections in the tennis world in search of a job at a tennis club. I had spent the previous summer working at Orchard Valley, a small tennis club near Detroit, and through that position I had made a friend named Mickey Grey. I made plans to return to Orchard Valley after our wedding the next year, but it was only a summer club, so we still needed a full-time job.

Mickey was a member at both Orchard Valley and an indoor facility called Square Lake Racquet Club in West Bloomfield, Mich., and he and several other Michigan friends recommended me for a tennis pro position there. We liked the area and the club, so I accepted the job offer and we started packing and planning for our move north as we simultaneously made last-minute wedding arrangements.

Since we were hundreds of miles away Mickey had been doing legwork for us up there, and when he found an apartment for us we paid the security deposit and the first month's rent. We were ready to hit the road right after the wedding, but then the day after our ceremony I received a phone call from Mickey that threatened to upend everything we had planned.

He told me there was a problem with the apartment—the one we had already been approved for and paid a sizable amount of money to reserve. Evidently, Mickey told us, the owner of the complex had learned that he was about to lease to an interracial couple and pulled the plug on the whole agreement. So much for transitioning to a more progressive, tolerant part of the country.

Of course, the apartment manager couldn't come right out and say that he was refusing us because of our race, so he improvised, saying we had falsified our application. The whole thing brought me right back to Bonnie Logan at the 1958 USLTA Junior Nationals when we were ten years old, having her trophy snatched away from her because they tried to convince people that this little girl had intentionally misrepresented her age on her tournament application. It's amazing how often racist people uncovered supposed "paperwork problems" from educated black citizens.

We were frustrated and unmoored; the rug had just been pulled out from under us just days before we were to make the long trip up to Michigan. With the hardships I had been subjected to throughout the years, I can't say I was surprised, but our friend Mickey was indignant. It was his recommendation that had helped lead me to the job and the apartment, and he couldn't believe we were being treated this way. Mickey had a number of well-positioned friends in the West Bloomfield area, so he started to rally his troops, especially from the legal profession.

By the time we had arrived in our new town, Mickey had consulted with several civil rights lawyers and assured us that we had an airtight case. An attorney from the Michigan Civil Rights Commission told us that it was the best case he had ever seen. Mickey told us, "We're going to sue him for everything he has. By the time this case is resolved, you're going to own all of West Bloomfield."

Of course, I had always been a fighter, so all of that sounded good to me. It was gratifying to have Mickey and many of his other white friends from the community on our side. Remember, Jo Ann and I had been married less than a week when we found ourselves in a legal battle that quickly became national news. We started out marriage out fighting against the world; that was our honeymoon. We hit the ground running.

We stayed with Mickey and his family for the first few days, and then a local hotel owner who was a friend of Mickey's offered us the bridal suite for free until we could find a new home. Despite the indignity the apartment complex owner had made us suffer, I was encouraged by the general spirit of inclusiveness in West Bloomfield and the embarrassment many of our new friends up there felt when they learned about our less-than-hospitable welcome. We started receiving daily letters from people in the area, new neighbors who wanted to let us know they were glad we had moved there. They told us, in their words and by their actions, "This is not who we are."

While we met with lawyers to consider our next steps, we started to visit other apartment complexes, because even if the original owner was forced to capitulate we knew we would never live in a place governed by hate. Every time we pulled up to a new leasing office, the manager would come out and meet us at our car. Everyone was extra hospitable and reassuring, and within three weeks we had moved into our new place.

As we got settled in and I started my new job, we still had a lawsuit to consider. The local attorneys, excited about the case that they considered a slam dunk, were anxious for us to pursue justice and to receive a hefty payout in the process. Black people in America were being harmed by discriminatory housing practices every day, and we could be a key catalyst for change in providing housing, a basic human right, to people of all races.

I was pumped up about it, but it soon became clear to me that Jo Ann was less enthusiastic. Finally one day, when I told her that we had an airtight case and we could be awarded a lot of money, we had a memorable exchange that showed me the measure of my new wife's character.

"I don't want his money," she said.

I was stunned. "What do you mean? We have a million-dollar lawsuit here."

"I just want to make sure this doesn't ever happen to someone else. We were fortunate. It would have been so much worse if we had already packed the U-Haul, then pulled into the parking lot and found out they weren't letting us move in.

"No, we're going to get this guy."

"All I want to do is protect others, get back the money we've already spent, and call it a day."

I looked at her like she was crazy, and every once in a while I still joke with her about it. "Imagine what kind of cars we would be driving if we had won that huge lawsuit!" I'll tell her.

But of course, she was right. We settled the case for a small amount of money to reimburse us for the rent and the deposit and to compensate for the mental anguish we had experienced. I found out later from Mickey that the attorney had turned the tables on us in the settlement and he didn't advocate for us well, so we received less money than we should have.

But in spite of that, Jo Ann took the high road, wanting to resolve things quietly and move on with our new life together. That's more than a million-dollar judgment any day. She doesn't have any regrets whatsoever when she tells the story. "There's just evil everywhere," she says. We still shake our heads over the fact that we left the Tennessee mountains (not exactly a progressive place), where our interracial wedding went off without a hitch, and ran into trouble in the suburbs of Detroit. At that point, Jo Ann and I realized that our life together would never be boring.

I had been coaching tennis on a part-time basis since my high school years, when I had the opportunity to work with kids back in Wilmington when I was home on breaks, and I was blessed with rich summer opportunities at the Don Kerbis Tennis Ranch and Orchard Valley. But the Square Lake job was significant because it marked my first full-time tennis coaching position, and I realized how much I loved identifying potential and coaxing it out of my students. I had a passion for teaching others, and I loved the challenge of taking the most uncoordinated, inexperienced person at that club and transforming that unlikely athlete into a tennis player. I've always understood, in part because of my own dedicated mentors, that everyone fundamentally needs someone who believes in them.

In addition to my regular lessons, I took the initiative to pay forward some of the generosity that my own pillars had given to me during my time at Square Lake. Fellow tennis pro Bob Love and I worked together to direct Michigan's junior development tennis team, a program that he developed out of his heart to provide high-level tennis opportunities to kids in Michigan who didn't have the means or connections to thrive in the sport. Just as Dr. Johnson had given his own home and backyard to me and other kids each summer so that we could become top competitors in the sport he loved, we created pathways for young people who were long on talent and short on privilege.

—⁂—

CHAPTER 15

World Team Tennis

Once we finally got moved into our own apartment and I settled into the routine of teaching tennis on a full-time schedule, Jo Ann and I were able to enjoy newlywed life in the Detroit suburbs. We had good friends in Bloomfield Hills, I was enjoying my job, and before long I had the opportunity to make tennis history as the first black player in an innovative new league called World Team Tennis.

In 1973, the year we got married and moved to Michigan, five men got together and decided to start a new league that would feature teams in sixteen U.S. cities. Everything about WTT was just a bit different from the traditional format in USLTA events; the court was painted with zones in different colors instead of being separated by white lines, players could substitute in and out during matches, and scoring was "no-ad," meaning that the winner didn't have to win by two points, and the winning team was decided by total games won, giving competitors an incentive to keep working hard even if they are losing a set.

When World Team Tennis was formed, it marked one of the times Arthur Ashe and I diverged on our tennis paths. I remember calling him and talking to him about the unique opportunity, but he wasn't interested in joining a team. Arthur preferred traditional tennis with the tried-and-true rules and scoring, but our careers were at different points by that time and I jumped at the chance to be a part of this historic venture. I would play for the Detroit-based team, and since the season would take place in the summer I would be able to compete while still working full-time at Square Lake Racquet Club.

The league's founders named George MacCall as its first commissioner and divided the teams into two divisions, Eastern and Western, and split each division into two sections. I was selected for the Detroit Loves, which played in the Central Section in the Eastern Division. I was the only black player in the nation competing in the WTT, and I was actually one of just a few players on the team from the U.S., since the Detroit Loves was loaded with Australian talent.

The Aussies on our squad included Phil Dent, who reached the Australian Open in 1974 (the year I played WTT with him), Kerry Harris, who won the doubles championship at the 1972 Australian Open, Pat Faulkner and Allan Stone. The biggest name on our roster, though, was American Rosie Casals, who won five Wimbledon and four U.S. Open doubles titles between 1967 and 1982 and reached two U.S. Open singles finals in 1970 and 1971. With depth like that, it shouldn't have surprised anyone when we won the Central Section championship with a record of 30-14.

We met the Pittsburgh Triangles in the first round of the WTT playoffs, but that team, which featured Vitas Gerulaitis and Evonne Goolagong, beat us 31-10 in the first match in Detroit and 32-17 in the second contest in Pittsburgh. After two seasons the owners of the team, Seymour Brode and Marshall Greenspan, realized that they were unlikely to draw enough fans to our home facility, Cobo Arena, to make a profit, so they sold the team to another ownership group that moved it to Indiana. The team competed in Indianapolis until 1978, when it folded.

My own involvement with World Team Tennis might have only lasted two years, but it was a significant chapter in my life for a host of reasons. I had the opportunity to be one of the inaugural players in a groundbreaking league that is still in existence to this day, and my presence allowed that league to be integrated from day one. I traveled all over the country to compete with WTT—Los Angeles, Washington DC, New York—and played alongside and against some of the greatest players in the history of our sports. I loved the team element of the league and the fact that it was founded with the intent of making tennis more of a spirited, exciting team sport for the fans.

At its best, WTT draws the fans into the competition in a way that most individual tennis doesn't, because it creates fan loyalty from the residents of the cities where the team is based. The vision of WTT was to bring tennis into a framework that made it feel more like professional baseball or football, and fans of the nine current teams still have the opportunity to follow tennis in that unique way today. In 2020 World Team Tennis was the first tennis league to resume operations after the initial outbreak of COVID-19.

When I retired from WTT it officially marked the end of my competitive tennis career, even though there would never be a day of my life after that when I wouldn't be working in the sport. My friends Mickey and Stu begged me to keep competing, even offering to pay for everything if I would join the USTA satellite tour. But my calling had changed. For years, as I tried to propel myself to the top of the tennis world, my own training and success on the court were top priority. But after World Team Tennis concluded I was no longer motivated to compete. I had a different purpose—to teach the game to anyone who was willing to listen and learn.

From the time I played in that first tournament under the watchful eye of my mother at the age of eight to those WTT playoffs when I was twenty-six, I spent a considerable percentage of every year competing on tennis courts throughout the nation. I'm proud of the accolades I collected during that time, which included:

- Two ATA men's doubles championships, 1964 and 1965
- Four ATA mixed doubles championships, 1967, 1968, 1969 and 1970
- Youngest male player ever invited to compete in the U.S. National Championships, 1964 and 1965
- Two National Prep Schools singles championships, 1967 and 1968
- NCAA quarterfinalist, 1972
- Who's Who in American College Sports for Tennis and Basketball
- 4 Ohio Valley Conference singles championships, 1968-1972
- 4 Ohio Valley Conference doubles championships, 1968-1972
- Section championship World Team Tennis, 1974

Over nearly twenty years of playing competitive tennis at a high level, I also had many opportunities to be an eyewitness to history, as my sport slowly made strides toward accepting players of every color and background. During every decade of my life I have seen a significant shift in the civil rights, both for black people in general in this country and for tennis players specifically.

When I started traveling with Dr. Johnson in the late 1950s, it would have been unheard of for us to stay in a hotel in the South, and we were turned away from a tournament that we had registered for because the country club didn't like the hue of our skin. By the time I started competing as a college player in the late '60s, we could travel, eat out and lodge without restriction, even if the unspoken racism in many areas still persisted. Then as we moved into the 1970s things opened up even more. Jo Ann and I would continue to experience roadblocks as we encountered ignorant people, but my personal trajectory in the world of tennis has traveled down an encouraging, if at times halting, timeline of progress.

Through my association with the American Tennis Association, prep school tennis, Division I college tennis and WTT, I made tennis friends all over the country. The people I have met through tennis have made my life richer and have helped direct me to new opportunities, just like my Michigan friends did when Jo Ann and I first moved to Bloomfield Hills. When the Detroit Loves moved out of town, another intriguing summer opportunity took its place—this one at a New York camp run by the man who would become one of the best-known tennis instructors in the country.

When I met Nick Bollettieri he was just getting started as a tennis coach and promoter; though he had only played high school tennis, when he dropped out of law school at the University of Miami he started teaching the sport, and in the 1960s he worked as the tennis director at a resort in Puerto Rico in the '60s. By the mid-'70s he was looking for new ventures, so he decided to start a summer adult tennis camp in Pawling, N.Y. and he hired me to run the camp.

I had the experience and the connections to help spark interest in Bollettieri's camp, and I enjoyed the opportunity to teach in a new setting and to help him build something from the ground floor. I spent two summers working in Pawling—a beautiful mountain area in upstate New York that actually reminded me of my college town in East Tennessee. I worked in two different facilities managed by Bollettieri—Quaker Hill and the adult tennis camp in Pawling. Quaker Hill was a private court primarily for members of the Kennedy family, and I found myself teaching tennis to some prominent people with outstanding connections. I enjoyed that side job and I got along well with Nick, who was actually setting his sights on starting a tennis empire far south of Pawling.

Jo Ann and I had spent four winters in Michigan, and for two Southerners that seemed like plenty, and we felt it was time for a change in surroundings. Because of those deep relationships within the tennis world I began to get job offers from tennis clubs throughout the country, but as I considered some new options I was also talking to Nick about his upcoming move to Sebring, Florida. Nick was a great salesman and I believed he could build something significant, so I accepted his offer to relocate to the Sunshine State to help lay the foundation for what would become the Nick Bollettieri Tennis Academy.

Our Detroit Loves team waiting to compete.

Our Detroit Loves team—Back row: Me, Kerry Melville, team owner Seymour Brode, Bob Love, Phil Dent, Butch Seawagen, Allan Stone. Front row: Rosa Casales, Trish Faulkner, Mary-Ann Beattie

As part of the Detroit Loves in the early '70s, I was the only black player on any World Team Tennis squad.

CHAPTER 16

Change of Plans

As Jo Ann I packed all of our belongings and loaded up the car for the long trip from Michigan to Florida, we had no way of knowing that the job I had accepted was with the facility that would become one of the nation's foremost sports training academies. We were prepared for a new chapter, but that anticipation of what awaited us in Florida was laced with a sense of the unknown. As it turned out, we should have asked more questions.

We had arranged for an overnight stay en route to Florida with the Maxeys, our dear friends from our college years who still lived in Johnson City, Tenn. We arrived at their house without incident, but as we were settling in I got a phone call from Nick Bollettieri that moved us from optimism to foreboding.

I was only thirty years old at that time, but even so I had been on the receiving end of far too many phone calls that started with the words, "We have a problem." On that day Nick used that dreaded phrase as a prelude to inform me about the concerns he had encountered to my hiring. In case anyone doesn't realize it when they focus on Disneyworld, Florida is still the deep South, and some of the players in Nick's new venture didn't think I needed to be a part of what they were building down there.

The Maxeys were very good friends; they had even sent their daughter Jan, who went on to play number one on the Vanderbilt tennis team, to live with us in Michigan for a while, but even so this situation was a bit awkward. We went from stopping for a quick night on our trip south to becoming the houseguests who might never leave—no job, no idea of which direction we should point the car next. But they were incredibly gracious and kind, telling us, "Listen, don't worry. Stay here as long as you need to." So we settled in for what turned out to be two or three weeks, using that time to fully investigate the situation in Sebring and decide our next steps.

It was never clear to me whether the people at Nick's new academy objected to the fact that I was a black tennis instructor or to my interracial marriage, (although it was probably the fact that my wife was white, since they knew I was black at the time they hired me), but at the end of the day that distinction didn't matter. Neither the color of my skin or the status of my marriage was ever going to change. Nick didn't completely close the door to my hiring, but he did tell me that we would definitely to stay in different housing than originally planned, away from the other tennis pros. This "new opportunity" was becoming more distasteful to Jo Ann and me by the minute. We realized that we weren't walking into a welcoming situation, and it didn't take long for us to resolve that Florida wasn't the right fit for us after all.

As I added this new and disturbing update to what I already knew from my work with Nick at the New York camp, I came to realize that the move to Florida wasn't in our best interest anyway. Sure, I could have been on the ground floor of what became IMG Academy, but I already knew that Nick and I had some philosophical differences. Nick was a businessman first, while I viewed teaching as a calling and didn't focus as much on the bottom line. There's no question in my mind that we dodged a bullet that day when our life was unexpectedly rerouted.

Remember that time, a week after our wedding, when our apartment lease in Detroit was pulled out from under us and Jo Ann took solace in the fact that at least we hadn't received the news after we had already packed the U-Haul and moved to the new place? Well, this time her fears from five years ago were fully realized. Here we were on our way to a new life, and we encountered not just a speed bump, but a brick wall, along the road we thought we were meant to travel. So we went back to the drawing board with our web of tennis connections, sure that God had a better path for us to follow.

Sure enough, soon another college friend came through, pointing us to a job opening at a place called Vic Tanny's Health and Fitness Club in Knoxville. Vic Tanny was one of the early health club pioneers, eventually opening more than a hundred locations throughout the nation, and the club in Knoxville was looking for a tennis pro. In yet another example of God paving the way for Jo Ann and I in a way that could never be called a coincidence, it turned out that the part-owner of that facility was Mike Lucci, a former NFL linebacker whom I had met when he was playing for the Detroit Lions. I met with him for an interview, got the job, and we quickly looked for a place to live in Knoxville, the city that would become our home for the next thirty-six years.

Once we were relocated in Knoxville, I jumped in teaching at Vic Tanny's, quickly making friends with my students and their families and, as I always have, building my reputation on the basis of excellence and strong relationships. I remember one member threatening to quit when she found out her child would be taught by a black man, but she relented when we got to know each other and she saw my effectiveness as a coach. I was able to win over parents like her and I made some quick friendships there, but the stable season of my new job only lasted a few months. Before long we hit another roadblock constructed by racial prejudice and envy. The general manager at Vic Tanny's had a problem with me, both because of the color of my skin and my growing popularity, which threatened him. He started spreading rumors about me that were in direct opposition to the opinions of the people in my growing support system within the club.

It was yet another unwelcome interference as Jo Ann and I tried to build our life together in a new city, as it soon became clear that I didn't have a future at Vic Tanny's. But this time we agreed that changing our location wasn't the answer. We wanted to stay in Knoxville, and the connections I had made during my short stint at Vic Tanny's made that possible. Ann and Bill Thompson, friends who were members at Vic Tanny's, had a private tennis court, and so they came to me and said, "Don't go anywhere. You need to stay here. Don't worry about a thing. You and Jo Ann can use our court to teach all the lessons you want." Soon I had a booming business on that private court, with students coming and going all day, every day. That was a sliding doors moment for us; we probably would have gone back to the job hunt and moved somewhere else, but because of the Thompsons' vision and generosity we made our home in Knoxville and stayed for three decades.

And so I established my own coaching business at that private court, and I know for a fact that I pulled students away from the club where the general manager had pushed me out. I would pursue other tennis opportunities in Knoxville in the future, but I stayed connected with that family and their court for years. That series of events was proof positive that investing in people, and maintaining our trust in the Lord, is the best way to go through life. We continued to accumulate evidence that people will let you down, but God is faithful and He will keep opening the right doors.

With yet another conflict fueled by ignorance behind us, Jo Ann and I settled back in Tennessee, the state that had formed the foundation of our early relationship. We had been married five years when we moved to Knoxville, and at that point I knew two things with certainty. First, I had been right about the inner strength of the woman I married. Second, now that Knoxville was finally starting to feel like home, we knew it was time to chase one of our most precious dreams—the dream of becoming parents.

I worked with Nick Bollettieri at his New York camp, but plans to help him start his tennis academy in Sebring, Fla. were derailed.

CHAPTER 17
Knoxville

We always knew that we wanted to have children, but in the early years of our marriage we were working through the upheavals that came our way because of racial prejudice as we figured out where we wanted to settle down. It took a while, six years to be exact, before we felt like we were ready to bring a child into the picture. Once we were established in Knoxville, we knew that, despite our fears, it was time to expand our family.

Some of those fears were the same reservations every new parent has, about keeping a child safe and raising them with the right values. But because of the unjust treatment Jo Ann and I had experienced over and over again in our young marriage, we had our own unique fears for our future children as well. If interracial marriages were so socially unacceptable that we would be denied apartments and jobs, what opposition and unkindness might our children face?

We were all too aware that while we had chosen this path with our eyes wide open, our kids would be forced to navigate a difficult road that they had inherited. But despite all of those dynamics, we never considered a world where we wouldn't have kids. We would teach them, as we were taught by our parents, about a God who loved them and had a plan for their lives, a sovereign God who would guide and direct them no matter what they encountered in the world. We would teach them to make a difference for good in this world.

We were ecstatic on September 20, 1979 when our first daughter Celeste made her entrance into the world. During Jo Ann's pregnancy, when we discussed names, I was emphatic about my wish to honor the woman who had done so much to encourage me as a young man and as a tennis player—Celeste Eaton. Our firstborn daughter's namesake was courageous and kind and full of grace, and now that our Celeste is an adult it's clear that she has grown into her name in every way.

Just thirteen months later, on October 6, 1980, our second daughter Jennifer was born, completing our family and giving us a set of "Irish twins" who grew up as best friends and sisters. It seems like Jennifer was in perpetual motion from the day she was born. It was a major challenge to get her to sleep through the night, and she was always running and climbing with a gigantic grin on her face. She certainly kept us on our toes.

As the girls got a little bit older and we brought them everywhere in a double stroller, people usually thought they were actual twins. From the time our girls were born until they started school, Jo Ann stayed home with them— homeschooling them for one year and then teaching preschool when they started going to school outside the home.

Our girls took after me in terms of their athletic abilities; they both played tennis until they were twelve or thirteen, but each had to find her own way with the sports they were passionate about. Celeste had a successful college career in track and field at Marshall University, and Jennifer made her mark at the University of Missouri on a basketball scholarship before transferring back to play at Tennessee Tech. They worked hard in their athletic pursuits and in their classrooms, and I'm proud to say that we never had to pay a dollar for college because of the scholarships they earned.

As our daughters were growing up and trying new things in school and sports, I continued to work in various sectors of the Knoxville tennis world. Spending more than three decades in one city allowed me to develop strong connections in the community and become not just a tennis coach, but a leader and an innovator on the city's sports scene at large. The truth is, I've never been content to focus on just one challenge at a time. I've always been a visionary with a tremendous amount of energy, so if I don't have my hand in three or four initiatives I feel like I'm wasting time. Starting with my one year at Vic Tanny's and then transitioning to the lessons at that private court, I progressively expanded my network and walked through new doors as they opened to me.

While I was teaching privately, I accepted an offer to become the tennis director at the Westside YMCA. Then, in 1988 someone from the City of Knoxville approached me and asked if I would become the city tennis director. That role would allow me to oversee a team of seven instructors at a big multicourt facility, and I couldn't resist the challenge, but I didn't want to quit working at the Y. So, in my typical way, I did both jobs at the same time. I had quit teaching private lessons, but my days were slam full as the top of the tennis food chain for a large city and a large YMCA at the same time. I was content, but that doesn't mean I wasn't always looking for new opportunities. When a small country club called Beaver Brook offered me a position as the tennis pro, I accepted that job, too.

Early in my time as the city tennis director, I launched a program offering free tennis lessons to any child living in the city, hoping to expose them to the sport that had so captivated me when I had finally been allowed to walk through the hallowed gates of Dr. Eaton's backyard complex at the age of five. As I worked with a variety of Knoxville children I noticed that they asked me about my time playing with greats like Chris Evert and John McEnroe, but that they were unaware of the giants like Althea Gibson and Arthur Ashe, my pillars, who had paved the way for them to excel as black tennis players. In offering free lessons to all comers, I had a goal that has continued to drive me through a lifetime of tennis education—to give black children the same exposure to tennis that they get to basketball and football and to educate them about the heroes who paved the way for them.

There actually was a period in the nineties when I was juggling all three jobs—the Westside YMCA, the City of Knoxville, and Beaver Brook Country Club. It didn't take long for me to realize that I couldn't sustain that workload, so I quit the city job and continued at the Y and the country club. After several years of coordinating the tennis programs at those two sites, I had another attractive offer at Fort Sanders Health and Fitness Center, a large facility connected to the local medical center. Fort Sanders had everything—eight outdoor tennis courts, four indoor tennis courts, a racquetball facility and every other type of fitness and sporting equipment you can think of.

I had a range of opportunities to teach lessons as a tennis pro in Knoxville, but those jobs make up only a slice of my involvement in the tennis world through those years. Through our church, Cedar Springs Presbyterian, I participated in sports ministry trips to Nairobi, Jamaica, and Mexico, where I taught tennis to children all over the world. We traveled down non-existent roads to the African bush to play tennis on packed dirt and to share our faith with the people there. But I learned more about Jesus from the people I met in tiny Jamaican, African and Mexican villages than we ever could have taught them. I was amazed and encouraged by their deep faith and their joy, and those are some of the most inspired church services I have ever attended in my life.

I also made a name for myself, and helped inspired countless young players throughout the Southeast, by organizing exhibition matches featuring well-known tennis professionals from around the globe. I put together my first tennis exhibition in the early eighties, when I brought in Billie Jean King and Hana Mandilikova to compete at the Stokely Athletic Center at the University of Tennessee. That first match drew big crowds, because Billie Jean and Hana were nationally ranked, and I soon realized that sports fans would pay to watch top tennis talent in person. I contracted with Pro/Serv, a Washington DC-based promotional company, to schedule many more tennis exhibitions—in Knoxville, Wilmington, Louisville, Baltimore, and multiple points in between. The full roster of tennis players that I hosted at these exhibitions reads like a world tennis hall of fame: Venus Williams, Serena Williams, Andy Roddick, John McEnroe, Ivan Lendl, Yannick Noah, Bryan Brothers, Katrina Adams, Martina Navratilova, Chanda Rubin, John Isner, James Blake, and of course my old friend Arthur Ashe.

I'm incredibly grateful that I had the opportunity to expose so many people to tennis of such a high caliber, but during my busiest years in Knoxville tennis was actually just one piece of the puzzle. By combining some of my connections with plenty of creativity and hard work, I also became the point person for a host of exciting events in my second-favorite sport: basketball.

One point of intersection between my tennis and basketball initiatives came through Pro/Serv, with whom I partnered to organize exhibitions for both sports starting in 1983. But even before that agreement, I took the lead for an All-Star basketball game in Greensboro that featured such greats as Julius Erving, Artis Gilmore, James Worthy, Phil Ford, and Dale Ellis.

Some of the events I organized existed solely as a showcase for the greats in the sport, while others benefited worthy causes. In 1986, for example, I spearheaded a 3-on-3 basketball tournament in Knoxville to raise money for drug abuse prevention and education. The marquee guests for the event were John Lucas, who was playing for Houston, and Johnny Dawkins, who had just been drafted by the San Antonio Spurs after an All-American career at Duke, Buck Williams of the New Jersey Nets, and the GOAT himself, Michael Jordan, who was about to start his fourth season with the Chicago Bulls.

I was committed to the battle against drug abuse because I had seen drug addiction take down several of my good friends who were also gifted athletes, men like former NBA star John Lucas, who was also a standout tennis player at the University of Maryland and one of my summer teammates at Dr. Johnson's Lynchburg summer ATA program, as well as my old doubles partner, Louis Glass. In an article about the benefit in the *Knoxville News-Sentinel,* I told sportswriter Chuck Cavalaris, "When I heard Lucas had been kicked out of the NBA, it all hit home. Here is a guy I grew up with, one of my best friends, and he picks one path and I choose another. The main thing that saved me was my faith in Jesus Christ and the strength that gives me."

In 1989 I was the event manager for a different type of 3-on-3 tournament when Knoxville was selected as a host city for Hoop-It-Up, a national competition series that was held in eighteen cities throughout the country. Each local winner advanced to the national Hoop-It-Up Tournament in Las Vegas, so the competition in Knoxville was fierce. Pat Summitt and Wade Houston, the head coaches of the women's and men's University of Tennessee basketball teams at that time, served as the honorary co-chairs, and we also organized an exhibition game between the Los Angeles Lakers and the New Jersey Nets to coincide with the event.

But amid the excitement of Hoop-It-Up and big-time NBA stars coming to my exhibitions, my most unique basketball venture involved an innovative basketball shooting machine called the Tornado. I was in Dallas at a convention for Hoop-It-Up organizers in 1989 when I first saw the Tornado in action; it was a tall, motorized pole with four goals facing north, south, east, and west, and it would spin while shooters would try to land baskets. That convention in Dallas was full of booths and vendors, but it seemed like nearly everyone there was crowded around the Tornado, and as I watched those baskets turning the wheels in my head started turning, too.

I weaved my way through the crowd and found George Bass, the inventor of the machine. He told me that only three Tornado machines existed in the nation, and when he saw how engaged I was by it he offered to sell me one. If I bought it, I would have exclusive usage rights to a large region in the Southeast. I called Jo Ann to run the idea by her, and by the end of that day I was the proud owner of one of the country's three Tornado basketball machines.

When I got back to Knoxville I spread the word about my new unique basketball machine, and soon I was in demand—providing the entertainment for halftime shows at basketball games, drawing customers to grand openings at car dealerships, visiting school assemblies, even showing up with the

Tornado as a special guest at birthday parties. The Dollywood theme park rented the device from me for three years, and during the ten years that I had the exclusive rights to travel with it, I carried the Tornado all over the South, meeting all kinds of people and giving them a new basketball experience.

Like the Tornado, I never really sat still, but I had a good time during those years as I literally kept countless balls in the air—tennis balls on the courts I managed in Knoxville, tennis balls and basketballs at big-time exhibitions and the basketballs that flew around during the annual Hoop-It-Up tournaments and at the array of Tornado exhibitions I was invited to make. Our girls grew from babyhood through the teenage years to young adulthood during our time in Knoxville, and we were invested in the community and busy doing worthwhile things. But even through that flurry of jobs and side gigs, there was one lifelong dream that I was still reaching for—one that had been denied time and time again because of persistent racial prejudice in the city I called home.

In 1980 at a fundraiser for disadvantaged youth in Knoxville.
From left Denver Broncos quarterback Craig Morton, University
of Tennessee basketball star Larry Robinson, Arthur Ashe and me.

Arthur Ashe and I pose after a fundraiser event and coach's clinic at the
YMCA in Knoxville in the '80s. I was the tennis director at the Westside
YMCA and I invited Arthur in as our speaker.

John Esner, Caroline Wozniacki, Caitlyn Simpson, Serena Williams, Andy Roddick at an exhibition I organized in Knoxville

Mike and Bob Bryan with Jo Ann and our daughter Jennifer at an exhibition in Knoxville

CHAPTER 18
Arthur

It was a cold February day in 1993 when I was called out of an indoor tennis lesson at Pellissippi State Community College to take one of the saddest phone calls I have ever received. Arthur Ashe—my hero, big brother and mentor—had died of AIDS-related pneumonia at the age of forty-nine. I didn't have any idea how to process this tragedy. If anyone deserved to live a long life, to keep rewriting history and making a difference in every community he entered, it was Ashe.

His untimely death was the last chapter in what was, without debate, one of the most extraordinary lives ever lived in this country. If he had only collected accomplishments as a tennis player, that would have been enough to make him into a legend. After all, he was the first African-American man (and at the time of this writing, unfortunately still the only one), to win the singles titles at the U.S. Open (1968), the Australian Open (1970) and Wimbledon (1975). He also won the doubles titles at the French Open in 1971 and the Australian Open in 1977, and he was captain of four victorious Davis Cup squads.

Arthur would have continued to electrify the tennis world, but in 1979, when he was only thirty-six, with no health problems, he suffered a heart attack. He underwent quadruple bypass surgery later that year, and in 1980 he retired after suffering chest pains again while running. In 1983 he had to go in for a second bypass surgery, and in standard operating procedure for such a surgery he was given donated blood. It would be five years before he would receive the shattering news that he had contracted the HIV virus from that blood transfusion.

Because AIDS was so widely stigmatized at the time, Arthur kept his diagnosis quiet, but in 1992 he revealed it publicly and, in typical Arthur fashion, remade himself into an energetic, informed activist fighting for the funds to cure the terrible disease that he found himself battling. He spoke to the World Health Organization and created his own foundation to raise support for AIDS research, adding to the advocacy work he was already doing for causes like American civil rights, apartheid awareness and fair treatment of Haitian refugees. As I learned that long-ago day when I wanted to lash out in anger at the tournament officials who were trying to make him play a crucial match directly after his first one, the secret to Arthur's power as an activist was his ability to listen and offer grace, but to stand firm for what was right without wavering.

While I grieved the man who had taken me under his wing when I was just nine years old, headstrong and homesick and desperate for the support my fifteen-year-old mentor provided, the world mourned my friend too. His death was national news, and Gov. Douglas Wilder of Virginia ordered that Arthur's body would lie in state in the Virginia State Capitol in Richmond, Arthur's hometown.

The wake in the capitol building was scheduled for February 5, 1983, with the funeral service to be held the next day in the Arthur Ashe Jr. Athletic Center, the facility he had founded to provide athletic opportunities to at-risk kids. Along with a handful of people who were household names in the worlds of tennis and politics, I was asked to serve as a pallbearer and to deliver a eulogy at the service.

My daughters were twelve and thirteen when Arthur died, but that trip to Richmond stands out as one of the most distinct memories in each of their minds. When we went to the viewing at the Virginia State Capitol, we paid our respects and then stood in the background to watch as a seemingly endless line of people filed through that historic building. While we watched, Jo Ann and I whispered to our daughters of a life well-lived, of the accomplishments and character who, despite the prejudice he faced, made such an impact that he was honored in such a way. It was important to us that Celeste and Jennifer understand the greatness of the man, the potential of one person to make such a pronounced difference in the world.

On the next day the funeral service was scheduled for 1 p.m., but people started arriving at the athletic center at 6:30 a.m. in hopes of getting a seat. It didn't take long for all 6,000 seats to be filled, with more mourners gathered outside the building. I lined up with the other pallbearers, and I just remember feeling like that walk to the front of the hall was endless, that I couldn't bear the weight—literally or figuratively—of losing the man who had provided guidance and support for every major decision in my life since the age of nine.

As we marched forward, I remembered those early days packed into Dr. Johnson's Buick Roadmaster, traveling to tournaments even though we weren't sure if the facility owners would turn us away at the club gates. I remembered Arthur telling me, "Lendward, you're not playing for yourself. You're playing for the future of other players," when he was treated so unfairly that day in 1961. I remembered seeking his advice about accepting the prep school opportunities, about playing World Team Tennis, about the professional jobs I had taken in Michigan and Tennessee.

Arthur had been on the receiving end of those and so many other telephone calls I had made over those decades, and Jo Ann and I have treasured memories of visiting he and Jeanne at the Doral Country Club in Miami each year to help them lead an annual holiday clinic. His brother Johnnie was also one of my closest friends. It was a strange thing to hold so many precious, personal memories of a dear friend, even as the whole nation remembered him and found ways to memorialize him through gestures like the beautiful bronze statue on Richmond's Monument Avenue and the Arthur Ashe Courage Award given annually at the ESPYS.

Atlanta mayor Andrew Young, activist and politician Jesse Jackson and former New York mayor David Dinkins all took turns at the podium after I spoke of my memories of Arthur. I recounted our meeting and his importance as a pillar of my life and a transformational force in the tennis community and beyond. Dinkins, a tennis player himself who got to know Arthur through the Ashes' time living and serving at-risk youth in Harlem, captured him well when he said, "It is said that service for others is the rent we pay for space on earth. Arthur Ashe left us paid in full. May he not look down and find any of us in arrears."

The early nineties were marked by grief for me and others who had been influenced by the black tennis community, as Dr. Hubert Eaton died in 1991, two years before Arthur. Dr. Eaton's death did not come as a shock—he had suffered from Alzheimer's and had been in decline for some time—but of course he had been a second father and an inspiration to me since I was five years old, and his impact on the Wilmington region, the national tennis community, and individuals like me was immeasurable.

Toward the end of his life, Dr. Eaton kept in close contact with my mom and other family members who still lived nearby, and as his memory and awareness declined because of Alzheimer's he would frequently wander away from his house and find his way to my mother's home on Ann Street. She would call his son, Dr. Hubert Eaton Jr., to let him know he was safe, and then they would sit and visit on the porch for a while. It's so interesting to me that he often ended up following that path to my house—the same life-changing route I walked with Mr. Jackson in reverse that day in 1953.

On September 5, 1991, the day after Dr. Eaton's death, the *Wilmington Star-News* wrote a tribute to him that stated, "Dr. Hubert A. Eaton Sr. may have done more to change Wilmington for the better than any other person in decades." After outlining Dr. Eaton's tireless efforts to end segregation in education, health care and recreation facilities, the article went on to say, "Dr. Eaton didn't fan old embers. He didn't take to the streets. He took to the courts. And one by one, he took down the barriers."

He took down one final barrier after he was gone, when his funeral service was held at Andrews Mortuary on Market Street in Wilmington. Funeral homes, like churches, are still one of the most segregated segments of life in the South, and I can't remember any other black funeral service being held at Andrews. But Dr. Eaton's life was honored there—a fitting memorial to the man who never stopped fighting to dissolve obstacles to black progress in his adopted city.

By the time we said goodbye to Dr. Eaton, his old friend and fellow tennis trailblazer Dr. R. Walter Johnson had already been gone for twenty years. Two years after Dr. Eaton's death we lost Arthur, who perhaps more than any other tennis player had taken a place in the national spotlight because of the boost he had received as a teenager from those early tennis pioneers.

Althea Gibson lived for ten years after Arthur passed, and by the time she succumbed to respiratory failure in September 2003, her extraordinary life story included not only her history-making Wimbledon, U.S. Open and French Open titles, but also a stint as the first black woman on the LPGA tour. In tennis, in golf, in her work with kids and in her lasting legendary status as a tennis inspiration for women and players of color, Althea left an indelible mark on this country.

"For players like myself and a lot of other African-American players on the tour, Althea Gibson paved the way for us," Venus Williams said after making her U.S. Open debut in 1997. "Althea Gibson improved my life and the lives of countless others," said tennis legend Billie Jean King after her death. "She was the first to break so many barriers and from the first time I saw her play, when I was 13 years old, she became, and remained, one of my true heroines."

It is my most fervent hope that history will never forget the profound contributions of Dr. Johnson, Dr. Eaton, Mr. Nathaniel Jackson, Arthur, and Althea—my pillars. They changed the world, and not just the tennis community, with their courage, determination, and vision. I can't believe how tremendously blessed I was to call each one of them mentor and friend. One of the purposes of this book, and of the talks I give to the young tennis players who train at my court, is to pass down the power of their legacies and light a fire under a young person who might take that baton and blaze an extraordinary trail of their own. I loved these five friends deeply, and I thank God every day for their impact on me and for the part I got to play in each of their unforgettable stories.

—◊◊◊—

The statue honoring my friend Arthur
Ashe in his hometown of Richmond, Va.

When a major thoroughfare in Richmond was renamed Arthur Ashe Boulevard, I attended the dedication along with, far left, Johnnie Ashe, far right, Katrina Adams.

Our last picture together with Arthur Ashe: Bobby Davis, Arthur Carrington, Arthur Ashe, Bessie Stockton, me, Wilbur Davis, Edgar Lee, Vernon Morgan and Wilbur Jenkins.

CHAPTER 19

A Place of My Own

The door to my own tennis dreams, and my life's calling, was opened in 1953 because a visionary black man named Dr. Hubert Eaton had constructed his own tennis facility in his backyard in Wilmington, N.C. Four years later, I was granted access to more possibilities because of an invitation to another private facility owned by another visionary, Dr. R. Walter Johnson of Lynchburg, Va. So I think it's fair to say that the seeds of my dream to own my own tennis facility were planted in me well before I could have expressed them to anyone.

Starting in the early '70s with my teaching position in Bloomfield Hills, Mich., I took the countless hours of tennis instruction from my own pillars and poured them into my own students—adults and children, beginners, and intermediates, all who had been captivated in some way by the sport that had put me on such an unforgettable trajectory. My students improved, and I came to understand the power of influence held by teachers, coaches, and anyone who regularly speaks into the lives of others. It was a high calling, and even though I had a wide range of opportunities to teach in private and public facilities throughout Knoxville, I knew I could be even more effective in a club of my own.

As it became clear that Knoxville would be our long-term home in the eighties, I started putting out feelers—looking for locations, learning everything I could about loans and funding. Even as I held down three tennis jobs at the same time, I was doing my research and taking steps toward that goal. Knoxville was a big city with plenty of interest in tennis, and I knew that my club could succeed if I was only given the opportunity.

These weren't just vague dreams; I had a specific vision for my club in those early years. In 1983, just six years after we moved to Knoxville, I told the local paper, "One day I hope to have my own indoor multipurpose athletic facility in Knoxville…I would like to do some things for the youth of this area—help develop their talents in tennis like Arthur Ashe and Dr. Johnson helped me. If I can influence one kid, maybe he will help another."

But conceptualizing the place I would develop—the values it would represent, the team I would recruit, and the athletes who would train there—was easier than making it a reality. My journey toward opening a tennis club was dotted with potholes, detours, and roadblocks, many of which would certainly not have barred my way if I had been a white man. So often it was an exercise in frustration, as I pursued "the American dream" that was always just beyond my reach.

I knew that my chances of success would be multiplied if I brought in partners with the financial strength and the business experience to pave the way, and the first such partner who tried to help me reach my goal was Arnold Pohs. Arnold, who developed a successful cellular technology company and later sold it for $1.5 billion, had been connected with Nick Bollettieri in Nick's early days, when they were running tennis camps in upstate New York.

Arnold had impeccable financial credentials. He was well-respected and incredibly successful in the corporate world, and he even had his own seat on the New York Stock Exchange. He and I started meeting about the process of finding the property, securing the loans and putting together a business proposal, and we had an airtight plan. We had secured a guaranteed FHA loan, and Arnold was personally backing the finance plan. With his help, I put together a package that should have made any lender feel secure, but when we visited several banks in Knoxville we kept hearing excuses and leaving without a loan approval. In one case, a day that stands out to me when I remember the futility of this quest, we had even gotten pre-approval from the bank's corporate office in Nashville before we arrived for our appointment at the local branch.

But, of course, there was one major problem. I wish "A black guy and a Jewish guy walk into a bank in the Deep South" was the setup for a hilarious joke, but on that day in the early eighties such a scenario wasn't humorous at all. Arnold and I walked into the bank office and sat down with the chairman of the board. We had our proposal and all of our loan materials ready to go, and we went through our whole presentation with him. I'll never forget the next words out of the chairman's mouth, even though sometimes I wish I could erase them from my memory.

He looked up at me and said, "This all looks very good. Everything is in order. I don't want you to think we aren't approving your loan because you're black." Talk about saying the quiet part out loud! Arnold and I didn't wait around to hear anything else insulting. We stood up, I shook the man's hand and we left immediately. I knew that we couldn't go into business with someone who led with such ignorance.

We tried other banks, but every door was closed to us. It was like the bankers in Knoxville couldn't expand their mental horizons enough to understand why a black man and a Jewish man would want to open a tennis club together in Knoxville. It was discouraging, to say the least, but even if I was a bit deflated by the rejections I still held on to my dream and kept looking for new inroads.

My next potential partner came my way a few years later. We met because I had taught tennis lessons to his wife. He was a securities broker and a businessman, and he had been an investor in Hoop It Up and in some of my basketball exhibitions. I trusted him and I believed he had both the financial capital and the local reputation to help procure the backing for my club. He raised a large amount of money for the venture when things fell apart, and that partnership came to a sad end. I was back to square one. Less stubborn individuals than me would have thrown in the towel at that point, but I refused to give up. I knew I belonged in that business and I still had a vision for the club I wanted to build. Fortunately, finally, God brought the right friend along at the right time.

Tom and Nancy Cochran had been some of our dearest friends for years. Tom is like a brother to me. He heads up a very successful family business in Knoxville. He had been a sounding board for me for years as I vented my frustrations about my ongoing quest to open my own club. One day he said he wanted to help me realize my dream. He and I sat down and put together a plan, and we became co-owners of Centre Court Racquet Club.

On March 17, 2005, after twenty-six years of elevated hopes, broken promises, and tentative restarts, Tom and I—alongside our families—cut the ribbon at the groundbreaking of our new indoor tennis facility. Later that spring, at long last, I started teaching students at my own club. In an article about the event in the *Knoxville News-Sentinel*, I told writer Jimmy Hyams that the journey to that point had tried my patience in numerous ways, to the point where I doubted seriously if it would ever come to pass.

"I wondered if it ever was really going to happen," I told him. "'Is it meant to happen? You get frustrated, angry. 'Why can't it be done?' You just keep beating the bushes." Even though I conceded to Hyams that "things are meant to happen at certain times," I knew many of the events that had thwarted me could have been avoided. I was a victim of narrowmindedness, greed, and dishonesty through those long years, but I still felt gratitude that my club had finally come to fruition with the right partner.

We had planned for a unique facility that would be one-of-a-kind in the Knoxville area. Unlike many sports centers that were staged in old warehouses or built in warehouse-like buildings, my club had walls that rolled up so that players could be exposed to the outdoors even when a roof was protecting them from rain. In severe weather or snow, we could close the walls, but often they stayed open and gave the courts a special indoor/outdoor feel. We also had traditional outdoor courts on the property.

Because the building materials for my club came from Germany, however, the shipping process was delayed beyond what we had projected, so it took nearly six months for the building to be completed. When we finally opened in late 2005, we started selling a range of memberships and finally I was the captain of my own ship. I already knew most of my staff, since I was able to hire them over from other tennis facilities where we had worked together in Knoxville. Their desire to come to Centre Court with me was a vote of confidence in my leadership at my new club, where I was able to organize family tennis camps, charity exhibitions featuring stars like John McEnroe and a host of other programs to expose kids and adults to the sport. It was a long-awaited fulfillment of a dream that had been deferred over and over, a tangible reminder that God keeps His promises.

—⁂—

CHAPTER 20

Back Home

Little did we know, when our tennis club was finally operating in full swing in 2006 and 2007, that we were on the cusp of the most catastrophic recession in my lifetime. Of course, sports and leisure activities are the first things to go when someone needs to trim their budget, so our memberships dropped and we had to cut expenses considerably during 2008. We made it to the other side of the downturn, but like many other businesses in our industry we continued to feel aftershocks even when the economy rebounded.

As we were considering the long-term profitability of Centre Court Racquet Club, I was experiencing an unexpected stirring regarding my hometown. It all started in 2011, when I was invited to ride in Wilmington's Azalea Festival Parade and to be honored as a celebrity guest. The Azalea Festival is a huge multi-day celebration in Wilmington, and when I returned for the festivities that spring I was transported back to a vivid memory from my childhood.

I was driving to the downtown Hilton, where the parade organizers had reserved a room for me, and the nostalgia and emotion were so overpowering that I had to pull my car over on Third Street and wrestle with the tremendous contrast between past and present. I remembered sitting along that street with my parents, watching the parade and feeling rejected and disrespected by the white people standing around us. I was a little boy at a parade, and all I wanted was for the people along the parade route to give me a piece of candy, but no one handed me anything.

I wept as I considered this new dynamic. I was now a celebrity guest, invited to ride in the parade, with a separate VIP section cordoned off where I could sit and watch the parade after my ride. It was an honor, but of course I harbored no misconceptions. Even if many legal and social barriers for black people in Wilmington had been removed, racism still simmered beneath the surface. But despite the sting of my memories, that Azalea Festival marked the beginning of my conviction that God was calling me back home. As I told a reporter for the *Wilmington Star-News* several years later, "God just put it on my shoulders and made it very, very clear through a conversation with John Ashe, Arthur's brother, that, 'Lenny, it's time for you to come back home and to make a difference in this community that you were brought up in, to give back to young boys and girls in the way that so many people in Wilmington gave to you.'"

I wasn't yet sure how that vision would be realized, but after that spring 2011 trip I turned to Jo Ann and said, "Maybe it's time for me to come back home to make a difference in this town." We didn't start packing right away; it was another year—a year full of prayer, courage and a new resolve that came with starting over after thirty years in the same place—before we actually made the move to Wilmington. In the time between that parade and the arrival of the moving van, several significant things happened that would affect our new life in North Carolina.

The first involved the closing of a long-pursued chapter in Knoxville. When the right buyer came along we knew it was time, so in 2013 we sold Centre Court Racquet Club after less than seven years of running it. That was a bittersweet decision because of the dream the club represented, but it also gave extra fuel to our potential relocation.

The second thing that happened involved a Wilmington city park called Empie Park, a facility that had long included tennis courts but a place where I had never been permitted to play in my earlier years. In 2009 the city announced its plans to add sixteen new courts to the complex and to name it after Althea Gibson, the tennis legend who had spent four years of her life living and training with Dr. Eaton. Even though we were still living in Knoxville the city brought me in as a consultant on that project, and after the expansion of the park was completed, I learned from some Wilmington friends that city officials were looking for someone to run the tennis program there. That leads to the third major event that contributed to our Wilmington return.

That third catalyzing event was my friendship with George Rountree III, a white Wilmington lawyer who had known my family for years and, unbeknownst to me, had been following my tennis career for a long time. When I started reconnecting with people in Wilmington, hoping to find the right opportunity, some childhood friends of mine recommended that I call Mr. Rountree, because he was well-connected and they believed he would be interested in my vision for reaching underserved kids in the community. I asked my mom to call him since I knew he respected her, and after receiving her call he invited me to come to his office the next day.

When Mr. Rountree and I sat down to talk, he opened the conversation with, "First things first: Why aren't you in the Greater Wilmington Sports Hall of Fame?" Well, I had been living away for fifty years by that time, so I didn't know Wilmington even had such a hall of fame. I told him so, and he said, "Would you do me a favor? Get back to Knoxville and send me all of your biographical info as quickly as possible?" And that's how I became the quickest inductee in the history of the GWSHOF; I was welcomed into that honorary body just a few months later, as part of the class of 2012.

That was one of four halls of fame I was invited to join in less than a decade. In 2011 I was inducted into the North Carolina Tennis Hall of Fame, Cheshire Academy Hall of Fame, followed by the Wilmington honorary the next year, the Black Tennis Hall of Fame in 2014 and the Southern Tennis Hall of Fame in 2020. Despite the racist attitudes that limited my potential for achievement in a white-dominated sport, I achieved a range of recognition in my later years, which was gratifying. The honors were particularly appreciated because they shined a light on the work I was doing to elevate at-risk children through exposure to tennis and mentoring.

Around the time of my GWSHOF induction, after the sale of my club in Knoxville became official, Mr. Rountree and other supportive friends like Herb McKim and Harry Kraly helped to put my name out for a management contract to run the Althea Gibson Tennis Center. Herb and Harry were natural allies for me because of our history together, which dated all the way back to our early years as tennis rivals growing up in Wilmington. Even though our races kept us from playing against each other much in our early years, I was always aware of Herb and Harry we had a mutual respect for each other. I do remember, when I was a teenager, that Dr. Eaton and I faced Herb and his father in the doubles division of the city championship. They were frustrated back then by the racist restrictions that kept us all from competing.

And even if they were too young to do anything about those barriers, when I moved back and started seeking opportunities in Wilmington forty years later they were completely on board.

They had a unique understanding of what I wanted to create to bring tennis to less privileged kids in Wilmington, and they were there every step of the way supporting me. I'm so grateful for those longtime friends and allies, and they relished the opportunity to right a wrong they had identified so many decades before.

When I announced my desire to manage the Althea Gibson Tennis Center, what resulted was a series of tense city council meetings, back-room negotiations and media rumors that underscored the continued presence of racial prejudice in the Port City. We heard every lame excuse in the book as to why I wasn't the right choice to manage that center, when I had decades of experience coaching and running tennis facilities at every level. It was tough to face so much backlash; it felt like my hometown had never even known me. I felt such clarity in my calling to come back and teach tennis, and suddenly this controversy threw up a major roadblock, prompting Jo Ann and me to pray even harder for courage and direction.

It wasn't so much the actual city council members who were pulling the strings to black ball me and deny me the management opportunity, but the movers and shakers behind the scenes who clearly didn't want a black man in charge of the city's tennis program. In any city, particularly one of Wilmington's size, you'll find a small group of wealthy, influential people moving the chess pieces around the board. They aren't usually the ones running for office or giving quotes to the media, but their power is undeniable.

One particular episode from this time proves the lengths my opponents were willing to go to. Someone found an article about a different Lenny Simpson, who happened to be from my father's little hometown of Long Creek, who had a criminal record. This person sent the article, complete with a photo of the wayward Lenny Simpson, to the *Wilmington Star-News* and wrote, "Is this the person you want teaching our children?" It was comical; that person was so obviously not me. I'm not even sure if the newspaper ever corrected its mistake, but supporters of mine in Wilmington, like Mayor Bill Saffo, apologized for the poor behavior of their fellow Wilmingtonians.

After that firestorm, the obvious move would have been to stay in

Knoxville. It was our home, after all, and with a few exceptions, the people of Wilmington weren't exactly rolling out the red carpet for us. But Jo Ann and I remained convinced that God was directing us to Eastern North Carolina. One of the watershed moments came during another conversation with Mr. Rountree, who supported me through the whole city council debacle and has been a steady encouragement to me in the years since.

Frustrated with the brick wall that had been put in my path, Mr. Rountree said, "You know what, Lendward? You need to stick it to this town and tell them where to go, because they don't deserve your talent at all. Stick it to them. Leave, and never come back here." I replied, "I appreciate that Mr. Rountree, but this will never be 1898. They are not running me out of this town. I'm not going anywhere." He understood then that I wasn't going to budge about my plan to move back, and his strong support for me never wavered.

Mr. Rountree is a first-rate lawyer, well-respected in Wilmington and across the country. He has been a fighter for justice and a faithful supporter of many organizations in Wilmington that champion opportunities for those that lacked the benefit of being born with a silver spoon in their mouth. From that first meeting, he has been a huge supporter of One Love. I have sought his advice and counsel on many occasions, and I have the deepest respect for him as a man, a friend, and a mentor.

Another important friend to us through our rocky transition back to Wilmington was my mother's old friend—and Althea Gibson's former tutor—Mrs. Bertha Todd, a community leader who is highly respected by all types of people in this city. Mrs. Todd is, quite simply, a force; she is in her nineties now, has written several books about her experiences growing up in Wilmington, and has advocated for me at every turn. When my mother was still living she was reluctant to encourage me in my efforts to create a tennis program in Wilmington, because she was afraid I would be rejected. But Mrs. Todd always believed, and she put her influence behind everything I did.

I had actually created the Lenny Simpson Tennis and Education Foundation while we still lived in Knoxville, starting the organization out of the back of my Tahoe with a large personal investment and the gift of 400 tennis rackets from Head, the company that had sponsored both me and Arthur Ashe. I knew that no matter where we lived, I wanted an organization for service and charitable giving. But in the midst of so much change and a variety of conversations with people in Wilmington, Jo Ann and I saw the potential for the foundation to support a comprehensive tennis and academic enrichment program in Wilmington.

In early 2013, we uprooted from our home in Knoxville and followed the Lord's leading to Wilmington, moving in with my mom in my childhood home until we could find a place to live. Through the foundation, we announced the launch of our youth program and started looking for community partners. One of my most memorable meetings about this new outreach initiative came with Mark Sinclair, who at the time worked for the Wilmington YMCA.

We were in negotiations to run our tennis program out of the YMCA facility, and as we chatted that day Mark asked me, "And what is your program called?"

"The Lenny Simpson Tennis and Educational Foundation," I answered.

"That's a long name," Mark said. "I'm just trying to picture it on a T-shirt or a sign."

"Well, Arthur Ashe named his foundation something similar, and if it worked for Arthur it should work for us."

Mark thought for a minute. "Have you ever considered the name One Love?"

"Whoa!" I said, and I actually clapped my hands. "That's it! Mark, if the Y is ever dumb enough to let you go I want you to come over and see me."

I was immediately drawn to the name One Love because it evoked tennis and my love for the kids in the program while carrying a strong spiritual theme. My volunteers and I can love children well and help guide them only because of the one who is love—Jesus. As we experience His one-of-a-kind love, we can pass it on to those God puts in our path.

After adopting our new name, it was just a few days later when the Wilmington YMCA announced a reorganization, Mark's position was eliminated, and he showed up at my door, where I promptly hired him as the director of communications for One Love Tennis. Mark was an incredibly valuable part of our organization; he was the spark we needed to help grow our work, and he loved to tell the story of One Love to anyone who would listen. He moved out of town in 2021 to be closer to family, and he is missed.

Our move, and the establishment of our tennis, mentoring and tutoring program, makes up the first part of One Love's origin story in my hometown. Despite the setbacks I had faced when I first broached the idea of coming back, I had prevailed and founded an organization that was already making a difference in the lives of kids—kids who reminded me so much of myself sixty years earlier when I was just a little spy in a tree, waiting for my neighbor to come back around the corner with that cold Coca-Cola. But there was another crucial part of the story, one that would soon unfold and bring us back, in a beautiful full-circle scenario, to the place where I first held a tennis racket.

My One Love instructors and I pose with one of our classes of students at the Martin Luther King Center, one of our training sites in Wilmington.

I had the chance to speak after I was inducted into the Southern Tennis Hall of Fame in Atlanta in January 2020.

We took groups of One Love students to the U.S. Open every year for five straight years, and our group got larger each time. Here we prepare to board the bus for New York.

Me and Jo Ann at the ceremony for the NJTL Founders Service Award, which I was given by the USTA in 2019.

Academic tutoring is a key component of One Love's multifaceted approach to helping students succeed. Here Kay Dougherty, one of our faithful volunteers, tutors a One Love participant.

Every afternoon we lead tennis clinics either at Orange Street or other partner sites in the city. Here I teach a group of kids at the Martin Luther King Center.

CHAPTER 21

Full Circle

It had been more than fifty years since I had lived in Wilmington full-time, but by early 2013 we had officially made the move east and we were signing up more children every day for One Love Tennis. It was good to be back; I was grateful for the strong friendships I had made with community leaders and the important work God had given me to do there. But there was an elephant in the room, and it was located at 1406 Orange Street.

Even before we ever thought of relocating to Wilmington, I had visited Dr. Hubert Eaton's old house many times. Whenever we would visit my mother's house on vacation, I took our girls on a walk around the corner to show them the place where my life had been changed on a backyard tennis court. We looked through the gate and I tried paint them a picture of what that plot of land had once looked like in its prime, when Althea Gibson, Mr. Jackson, Dr. Eaton, and others were playing incredibly high-level tennis and then laughing and talking after their matches with cold bottles of soda.

It was bittersweet to go back, because every time I visited that house and yard I saw more deterioration. In 2002, eleven years after his father's death, Dr. Eaton's three children put the house on the market, and a local group had considered turning it into a daycare center. Ironically, my mother led the opposition to that plan and it didn't happen. Even at the time of the house's sale, it had been many years since anyone had used the tennis court, and after new owners came in the backyard started to look more like a jungle than a country club.

When we moved back to Wilmington we lived in my mom's house on Ann Street for about six months, so of course I saw 1406 Orange Street and its overgrown backyard regularly. I remember one walk over there in particular with my daughters Celeste and Jennifer and grandchildren Caitlyn, Bryce and Brayden shortly after we moved back. My grandson Brayden, the youngest, was three-and-a-half, and he was apt to imitate everything I did. That afternoon we stood on the edge of the property and surveyed the yard as I told them the story of those early walks around the corner and that first tennis racket courtesy of the legendary Althea Gibson. I stood with my hands behind my back and Brayden stood next to me, exactly the same way, and that day I distinctly remember thinking, "I have got to do something with this property." I knew it wouldn't be easy, but I just couldn't stand by and watch the place that had started me on my life's path and inspired countless tennis players become forgotten and neglected.

That night I turned to Jo Ann and I said, "I've got to do something about this property. This is a disgrace. This is a shame. Look what's happened to this iconic property, where world champions and other great tennis players trained? Why isn't there a tribute to the Eatons, who did so much for this community?" She said, "What do you want to do?" (Now remember, this is the woman who patiently agreed to let me buy a basketball machine called a Tornado.) I replied, "I don't know, but I have to do something."

Right around that time, we had our first fundraising luncheon for One Love Tennis. It was no accident that a couple named David and Carolyn McLemore were among the guests at that luncheon; I had met David shortly after I moved to Wilmington through my friend Jack Manock, who also attended The Hill School. David had been looking for a worthy cause to support, and that day when he heard me share my story and my certainty that God was calling me to intervene regarding the Orange Street property, he felt equally certain that he needed to help me. In 2016 David made a major gift to One Love—$200,000 and a fifteen-passenger van—that ignited our program and started to make me think that my big dream could be possible.

David's friendship was one of the most important ones of my life. Not only did he support One Love wholeheartedly, he wanted to learn about me personally and where my strength and perseverance came from, and of course I shared my faith with him. Through our times together he renewed his own faith in the Lord. When David died in August 2022 we grieved the loss of a great man, but we didn't mourn as those who have no hope, because we know that He is with Jesus and that his tremendous legacy lives on every day on Orange Street and beyond. God certainly knew what He was doing in allowing David and Carolyn cross our paths when we moved to Wilmington. Their partnership made all of the difference in elevating and encouraging our efforts in our new community.

We made an inquiry, and the owners of the house gave us an initial asking price that we thought was outrageous. David was a person who dreamed big, and he was determined to help find a way to help One Love buy the house so that the kids in our program could play tennis on the court where I had first swung a racket, but I knew that price was way too high and I didn't feel good about it. We had visited the house at least three times that fall, but the asking price didn't budge. We were still weighing our options as Christmas approached that year. We were visiting our family in Knoxville, just two or three days before Christmas, when I had a strong feeling that I needed to pick up the phone and call the owners, and it couldn't wait. I was confident that I needed to make them an offer that they didn't feel they could refuse.

I talked it through with David first, and then I made the call. I offered a lower price and told the homeowner that I would give them cash for the house—no mortgage, no hassle. If they would accept that offer, I told them, we would take the property "as is." They wouldn't need to address the structural issues that we expected were extensive. (Even though we had no idea how bad things really were.) I emphasized to them that I wanted to restore the home to its former glory because of its historical significance, and I hoped they would be swayed both by my mission and by the simple terms of my offer, which wouldn't require any extra work from them.

The lady who lived there said, "OK, I'll tell you what. Let me talk to my husband and my parents. In twenty-four hours she called back and accepted, and the deal was done. Thanks to the McLemores' partnership and my boldness in making that offer, I was the owner of 1406 Orange Street, and the phrase "full circle" took on new meaning for me.

I was initially thrilled, of course, to finally have possession of the property that had meant so much to me since I was a small boy, but my next thought was, "What in the world have I done?" The house needed extensive work, and the more we uncovered the more we saw that needed to be done. After David and I surveyed the situation thoroughly, we realized that our only option was to strip the whole place down to the studs and start over. It would take a considerable amount of time and money to bring the place back to top form, but we knew that our first priority was the backyard tennis court.

If a visitor had walked into that backyard right after we bought it, they wouldn't have been able to guess at the boundary lines of the tennis court where I had learned to play sixty years earlier. I knew where they were, but that was purely from memory, because that yard was more like a jungle than a tennis court, even though we eventually excavated one of the posts from the old tennis net. We hired contractors to clear out the grass and the weeds, resurface and reline the court and rebuild the net and the fence.

In addition to the McLemores' significant gift and other contributions from individuals and businesses in the Wilmington community, we also received $50,000 from Wilmington native and basketball legend Michael Jordan to aid in the restoration of the court, and the USTA also made a very substantial donation, which was an appropriate acknowledgement of the court's place in American tennis history. In April 2019, we held a ribbon cutting and dedication at the site, and the new clay court was officially open to introduce tennis to a new generation of Wilmington youth. Attached to the new fence was a plaque honoring the contribution of Carolyn and David McLemore, who had believed in my vision from the very beginning.

"We want to serve the kids who can't belong to country clubs, or afford expensive equipment, or travel to tournaments," I told Steve Tignor of Tennis. com at the time of the dedication. "We want this to be a catalyst to revitalize this neighborhood. People here know the history of this house, and we want it to be a positive example."

By the time our One Love kids were finally able to play at 1406 Orange Street, our program was well-established in the community. We had hundreds of kids learning to play in our clinics, our tutoring program was in full swing and we had established a select junior development program for the most promising players. I can't describe the emotion I felt when those young players I had formed such a strong connection with walked out on the court of my childhood and started to play. It was the vivid fulfillment of a dream that had, at one time, seemed impossible.

Speaking of things that once seemed impossible, in 2015 we found ourselves with access to the exclusive All-England Club in London, the same place where I had missed the chance to play because of an injury decades earlier.

It all started through our friendship with Jenny Spruill, an English native who played at Wimbledon in the late '50s and early '60s and eventually ended up in Hampstead, N.C. I met Jenny and her husband Jack when they attended the showing of the "Althea" film, directed by Rex Miller, a very accomplished filmmaker and producer, in Durham, N.C. at Thalian Hall in Wilmington. We talked briefly after the show and she shared with me her tennis history. We laughed about how small the world is. Jack and I met again later for lunch and we talked about them getting involved with my One Love program and the opportunities to screen the Althea documentary. He said to me, "Maybe you should show this documentary at the All-England Club (Wimbledon)? Jenny has close ties there and could serve as your introduction to the chairman of the board." Needless to say, I jumped at the opportunity.

After Jenny laid all the groundwork, I had a series of correspondences with the chairman of the board of the All-England Club. I explained Althea's powerful legacy and her lack of recognition at Wimbledon, where she had made history, and eventually I sent him the documentary. After he watched it he called me and said, "After I finished the documentary I was sitting in my office looking out at Court One where Althea competed, and I could just see her playing there. I think it's time for you to come over here and show the documentary to our members."

We did just that in 2015, crossing the pond with a group of eight that included me and Jo Ann, Jenny, One Love board members David and Carolyn McLemore and David and Kay Daugherty and Rex Miller, the director of the film. We got to take an exclusive tour of the club, seeing areas that few people ever get to see. We even sat in the luxury box where reigning British monarch always watches Wimbledon matches. We returned to Wimbledon in 2017 to give stroke demonstrations to local children at their learning center on the Wimbledon grounds, and now every year we get invited to attend Wimbledon and sit in the members-only area. Every time we make the trip, it's another chapter of a dream come true.

The Eaton House backyard was alive with activity again every afternoon, but it was nearly two more years before the house was ready for me and Jo Ann to move in. While the work continued, we enjoyed the condominium at Wrightsville Beach that we had rented shortly after we moved to Wilmington. After thirty years in the mountains, it was amazing to be so close to one of

North Carolina's most beautiful beaches, and even more so because I had never been permitted to set foot on that beach when I was growing up there.

When I was a child, the only beach that was open to black people was at North Topsail, which was about an hour's drive north from our house. Even though Wrightsville Beach was only ten minutes away, it might as well have been in another country as far as we were concerned. For years ordinances prevented black people from walking on the beach, the boardwalk, or even in front of the cottages where white people stayed, unless they were working in some capacity. I don't remember ever crossing the Wrightsville Beach bridge once in all the years of my childhood.

Jo Ann and I lived at the beach for eight years, until the house was finally completed in late 2021 and we were able to move in. With a historic plaque to the left of the front door honoring the home's rich history, and the sounds of tennis balls bouncing all afternoon, it didn't take long for us to feel at home in the place that held so many memories for me. The neighborhood had changed, but it would always be the place where Mr. Jackson had walked me through those gates, where I had run to the corner store for cold Cokes, where Aunt Ruth had marched us home when she thought we were out of line. And with One Love's commitment to community outreach efforts like our monthly food drives, we let it be known that, like Dr. Eaton had years before, we were dedicated to providing opportunities and growth not just through tennis, but by serving our neighbors in every way we could.

—⏀—

Side-by-side images, sixty years apart. Left, Dr. Eaton on his backyard court, and right, me on the same backyard court after we bought and renovated it.

My grandson Brayden copied my stance as we surveyed the property at 1406 Orange Street shortly after we moved back to Wilmington.

In 2018, we had the opportunity to take some of our players to the Fed Cup in Asheville, N.C.

I got the chance to dress as a "bobbie" at the All-England Lawn Tennis Club, site of Wimbledon. Every day I went up to them to joke around with them, and they finally let me try on their hat.

Watching a match on Center Court at Wimbledon in 2019.

The Center Court view from the Royal Box at Wimbledon in 2019.

The appointment of a Community Learning Officer in 2017 increased the opportunities for local schools and community organisations to visit Wimbledon with 20 free visits offered to local primary schools and a Family Fun Day held for local teachers and their families.

The Learning team hosted an off-site exhibition for the first time at the AEGON Classic in Birmingham. Inspirational Women in Tennis focused on former Wimbledon Champions including Althea Gibson, Billie Jean King and Venus Williams and local school children attended workshops linked to the exhibition.

During Black History Month, former US tennis player Lenny Simpson visited Wimbledon and gave a series of inspiring talks to 150 pupils from local secondary schools.

I was honored to be featured in the 2019 Wimbledon Year in Review publication for my talks to local schoolchildren.

One Love board members and other supporters join me in cutting the ribbon for our One Love Tennis Center on Orange Street in April 2019.

David and Carolyn McLemore have been some of my most faithful and generous supporters since I moved back to Wilmington. In 2019 they celebrated the ribbon cutting of the renovated court at 1406 Orange Street, which was named in their honor.

Our One Love students wrote forty letters to the USTA lobbying for a permanent Althea Gibson recognition at Flushing Meadows.

CHAPTER 22
Pillars

Every week in my hometown of Wilmington, operating out of the house that once belonged to my hero and mentor, I have the privilege of helping local kids discover their worth and God's purpose for their lives—through tennis, academic enrichment, community service, and more. This "full circle" chapter in my life is such a gift, especially since it allows me to take the values I absorbed from my own pillars and instill them into a new generation.

Due to health setbacks in 2021 and 2022, I've been forced to slow down for the first time in my life, and in my moments of reflection I'm full of gratitude when I consider God's faithfulness to me over the decades. My family is a daily blessing, my friends encourage and love me through everything, and I was blessed enough to cross paths with five of this country's tennis giants–men and women who profoundly shaped me into the man, coach, and mentor I have become. The fruits of their influence, and my efforts to shine a spotlight on their accomplishments, are illustrated vividly through the mission and works of One Love Tennis.

The advocacy, love, and determination of Dr. Hubert Eaton Sr. shine through every day as young people play tennis on the court that he lovingly built and shared with kids like me more than sixty years ago. It was the only tennis option I had available to me, and while times have changed and our students can play other places, we have created an environment that makes our court, and the program that surrounds it, more meaningful than any ordinary tennis program they might enroll in. Dr. Eaton was committed to education and to justice, and our own adherence to furthering those principles dominates everything else we do at One Love.

Sometimes, when one of us is out on the court instructing a child on the fundamentals of tennis and "getting it right," I can almost imagine Dr. Eaton sitting on the back porch with Celeste, smiling and watching new students of the sport that gave him so much joy. And when we collect hundreds of bags of food every month and give them out to our community as part of our monthly One Love Food Drive, we are paying tribute to the doctor who worked tirelessly throughout his life to serve the people around him.

Whenever I see potential in a young player and nudge them to develop that talent, I do so in the memory of my next-door neighbor Mr. Nathaniel Jackson, who was as generous with his tennis assistance as he was talented on the court. Without Mr. Jackson's persistence and kindness I never would have made it over to the Orange Street court in the first place, and whenever possible I pay tribute to him by reminding young people that nothing is impossible with the right mentors and a steadfast commitment to hard work.

I channel the energy and high standards of Dr. R. Walter "Whirlwind" Johnson when I challenge our One Love children to sweep the court with excellence after a lesson, to spend ten extra minutes working on a skill and to hold their heads high no matter what—even if they don't play their best or they aren't treated with the respect they deserve. I have lived my life with the steadfast brand of discipline that Dr. J instilled in me, and I have had the opportunity to pass that baton, reminding young people that there is always time to do something the right way and that a commitment to excellence pays untold dividends.

When I moved to Wilmington with a dream of running the Althea Gibson Tennis Complex and faced the same type of opposition that had tried to stop us in Michigan, in Florida and in Knoxville, I reacted with the grace that my friend Arthur Ashe had modeled when we were just teenagers and I wanted to go to battle over the way he was treated at the USTA Junior Championship in Kalamazoo, Mich. Arthur's example guided me as I developed into a man myself, and I continued to draw strength from him in my later years as I witnessed him face a devastating diagnosis with grace and courage. When I formed One Love in 2013, I looked to Arthur's powerful work as an advocate for AIDS research and awareness. He wasn't the first athlete to use his high profile to change the world for the better, but he has certainly spurred many athletes on, including his "little brother" from Dr. Johnson's summer program.

And of course, whenever I encounter a promising young player who might not believe in their abilities, or I encourage them to balance their hard work on the court with discipline in the classroom, I am honoring the great Althea Gibson, who came all the way from New York to North Carolina, far out of her comfort zone, because the two doctors told her it would set her up for greatness. And greatness, of course is what she achieved. Our One Love kids love to learn everything they can about Althea, because their hometown claims her as one of its own and she made history in the world of tennis and beyond. As the young people of Wilmington have embraced Althea's story enthusiastically, they have also become effective lobbyists in efforts to help cement her legacy.

First, in fall 2014, we led the One Love Tennis community to campaign the City of Wilmington to declare the first week of September as Althea Gibson Week. After that effort, I organized showings of the acclaimed documentary "Althea" in local elementary, middle, and high schools, with a Q and A following the film. Inspired by that retelling of Althea's extraordinary life, some students resolved that they needed to do more to honor her memory. We had already started a letter-writing campaign at One Love asking that a statue be erected in Althea's memory in Flushing Meadows, N.Y. at the site of her U.S. Open triumphs in 1957 and 1958, so a group of other young ladies I had taught joined in the campaign. A CBS crew even came to Wilmington around that time to feature One Love and our letter-writing campaign in the 2019 film "Althea and Arthur."

In 2018 we sent forty letters to the USTA, each detailing Althea's historic accomplishments and asking for a permanent monument to her prominence as a tennis and civil rights trailblazer. And when the Althea Gibson memorial was unveiled in Flushing Meadows a year later in April 2019, Jo Ann and I were there along with a group of kids from One Love Tennis, whose hard work and dedication to Althea's legacy had had a permanent impact on the way the game will be remembered. The statue unveiling made the trip extra special, but it was actually the fifth time we took our One Love players to the U.S. Open. In a tradition initiated by David and Carolyn McLemore in 2015, we went to New York each year to perform stroke demonstrations and assist with the coin toss before matches featuring the best players in the world. Also thanks to the McLemores, three of the bricks at the U.S. Open's Avenue of

Aces in Flushing Meadows were dedicated in our honor: One for One Love Tennis, one for Jo Ann and me, and one for the McLemores.

Our traveling group got larger every year; by 2019 when we saw the dedication of the Althea Gibson statue, we had forty people in our party. That was a most memorable, but chaotic day; just minutes after the unveiling ceremony outside the facility, we were expected to be on center court, where four of our kids had been invited to conduct the coin toss and our group had also been scheduled to give a stroke demonstration before the match began. But even though we were trying to be in three places at the same time, it's a safe bet that none of our One Love players will forget that experience.

It was through that letter-writing campaign that One Love developed a strong connection with Katrina Adams, the first black president, CEO, and Chairman of the Board, at the USTA and a highly competitive player in her day. Adams, who won more than twenty career double titles on the Women's Tennis Association tour, first visited us in Wilmington in 2017 for a fundraising banquet, and we surprised her by having seven of the girls from One Love read their letters out loud to her at the event. She returned four years later to teach a youth clinic and promote her book, "Own the Arena." Katrina has become a new inspiration for our young people who see in her life, and mine, the way tennis can help open doors to possibilities beyond their current imaginations.

The same year Katrina spoke at our banquet, I had an unforgettable opportunity to champion the tennis history that is so tightly woven in with my own. Ten years earlier I had been asked to consult on a traveling exhibit called "Breaking the Barriers" that traced the rich legacy of black tennis in the U.S., and in 2017 One Love was one of the sponsors that brought the interactive exhibit to Cape Fear Community College in Wilmington. The event, which coincided with the 100-year anniversary of the American Tennis Association, drew more than 58,000 visitors who had the chance to walk through and learn all about the greatness of each of my mentors and many more tennis greats who fought for respect and opportunity in the sport they loved.

Through the kids and parents who have come through the doors of One Love, our neighbors, our church family at Port City Community Church and so many others who have stood behind us in our work in Wilmington, we have reclaimed this city as home. I know without a doubt that our investment in the kids here has made a difference, and I've been gratified by acknowledgements of that commitment. In December 2020, I was just the third recipient in history of the Wilmington Star-News Media Lifetime Achievement Award, and over the eight years we have lived in Wilmington we have raised money for One Love outreach and community service again and again, always confident that our friends in Eastern North Carolina will give generously.

Even though I knew my Wilmington community believed in One Love's work, I experienced the support of "my people" in a new and profound way in March 2021, when I suffered my third and most severe stroke after also battling prostate cancer for eight years. I was in very serious condition for weeks, and Jo Ann and I believe fervently that the faithful prayers of our friends and family strengthened me. We also know that God wasn't finished working in or through my life.

After several days in the hospital and many months of therapy, I made a recovery that the doctors consider miraculous, and the work of One Love Tennis continued on. Neither a worldwide pandemic nor my own health problems would keep us from carrying out the ministry God has given us in Wilmington. And even if my speech and my movement was slower after the series of strokes, my platform grew because I had a dramatic story of God's faithfulness. I may have slowed down, but God is working double time because He does His most powerful work when we surrender to Him in our weakness.

In 2 Corinthians 12, Paul wrote something beautiful that describes this season of my life: *"But he said to me, 'My grace is sufficient for you, for my power is made perfect in weakness.' Therefore, I will boast all the more gladly about my weaknesses, so that Christ's power may rest on me. That is why, for Christ's sake, I delight in weaknesses, in insults, in hardships, in persecutions, in difficulties. For when I am weak, then I am strong."*

I have undeniably been through some hardships, starting with racial persecution during my tennis career and continuing through blocked business opportunities because of my race to my present medical struggles. I still wrestle with regret sometimes, especially when I watch a big tournament in Wimbledon and realize that I missed my one chance to qualify because of a pulled muscle. A white player of my ability during the 1960s or '70s would have had multiple roads to Grand Slam qualification, but for players like me the road was crazy narrow and the door was apt to slam shut at any moment. I wish I could have had the full access that my white counterparts were given.

I wish I could have seen where my unfettered potential could have led me.

But even though I do sit in those thoughts sometime, I am nonetheless certain that Christ's power has rested on me time and time again. He has been glorified even when external or internal forces have kept me down. I embrace the words that Paul wrote in 2 Timothy 4:7-8: *"I have fought the good fight, I have finished the race, I have kept the faith. Now there is in store for me the crown of righteousness, which the Lord, the righteous Judge, will award to me on that day."*

God is indeed writing a beautiful story through me, His story of faithfulness and grace, and my job is keep listening to His voice, loving my family well and serving the people around me. His love holds no matter what, and as a vessel for that love, that one love, I can walk in confidence knowing that He can use every event in my life, painful or ordinary or triumphant, for His glory.

The same is true for countless other young black men and women. Those that came before me and those who will follow. *"For I know the plans I have for you,' declares the Lord, 'plans to prosper you and not to harm you, plans to give you a hope and a future." Jeremiah 29:11*

—⁂—

Me and my girls: Jo Ann, our daughters Celeste and Jennifer and our granddaughter Caitlyn on the court at 1406 Orange Street.

For several years we have organized a community food drive every month for our One Love neighbors.

Here I am outside our house at 1406 Orange Street ready to distribute groceries on food drive day.

At the Fed Cup, one of the students from our One Love program had the opportunity to escort Serena Williams during a tournament event.

Our One Love students practice for a stroke demonstration clinic at the U.S. Open.

Our One Love group has had several opportunities to participate in youth events at the U.S. Open. Here we are in front of the South Plaza Fountains at Flushing Meadows in 2017.

In 2019 we were invited as guests of honor for the unveiling of the eighteen-ton Althea Gibson bust at the U.S. Open, a memorial that came about in part from our letter-writing campaign to the USTA.

After Bryce's basketball game in Charlotte with my son-in-law Tamar, my grandson Brayden, my daughter Celeste, and my grandson Bryce.

Joining me at the 2022 ETSU awards ceremony were Celeste, Lenny, Jo Ann's brother Mark Buchanan and her niece Laura Barr.

In 2022 I was selected to receive the Alumni Award of Honor by my alma mater, East Tennessee State University.

Bryan Daniels, me, and Dr. Brian Noland at the ETSU Outstanding Alumni Award Ceremony

Me and Jo Ann at the ETSU Outstanding Alumni Award Ceremony

Jan Maxey Stubbs, my daughter Celeste, me, and Jo Ann at the ETSU Outstanding Alumni Award Ceremony

Some thoughts and memories of Lenny Simpson from members of his inner circle:

CELESTE SIMPSON SLAY

Growing up we learned to pour our heart and soul into everything we did. We were taught to "do the right thing" and always carry ourselves with dignity and respect. My sister and I spent lots of time on the tennis court playing in my father's summer camps, clinics, and tournaments. I gravitated more towards track and field, but the lessons of perseverance he taught me carried over into my career.

My father inspired me to never give up, and I believe these same qualities allowed my father to accomplish so much in his life. He's a strong yet compassionate man, an amazing father, and a wonderful Grandad to his grandchildren. His undeniable love and support for all of his family is what I love the most about my father.

JENNIFER SIMPSON

My dad instilled in me hard work and dedication in everything that you do. I especially remember this when I played basketball and I had to shoot a thousand shots a day before I did anything fun. Also, he taught me never let someone tell you that you can't do something. "Simpsons never quit" is a family motto. I witnessed his determination to be the best tennis player he could be, no matter the obstacles he faced. His love for his kids and grandchildren is amazing. He is such a great talker—he could sell you anything and make you a believer of what he was selling.

My dad's legacy is literally one-of-a-kind. He grew up when racism was so bad, and he was taught by Dr. Johnson to be respectful no matter what. He has always been such a strong, loving, caring and passionate person. He is really a big teddy bear. I love my dad so much and I'm so proud of all his accomplishments. There is only one Lendward Simpson Jr, and he is my dad!

BONNIE LOGAN

When I met Lendward when we were young, twelve and thirteen years old. It was an exciting time for us. We had aspired to be the best in the world; That was our goal. We were very serious, which is probably why we got along so well. We had the same goal in mind. We wanted to be number one. We were kind of unbeatable in mixed doubles, but what we really wanted was to play together as adults in the professional ranks. It was a wonderful time when we were traveling up and down the East Coast and the Midwest as teenagers, playing in a lot of tournaments. Winning was so important to us, but we also wanted to make a great impression on the world, as we were representing our race.

I'm so proud of him because he went on to do so many great things in the sport. I tell him all the time that what he has done for tennis is so wonderful. It takes a special type of person to do the things he's done. I was down there in Wilmington for the dedication of Dr. Eaton's court, and I'm just so happy that his dream and goal came to life. For him to realize his goal is beautiful.

GEORGE ROUNTREE

I met Lenny when we were younger, because I was an acquaintance of his mother. When he moved back to Wilmington I became a supporter of his efforts to become involved in the Wilmington tennis community. From the beginning, he faced so much opposition. Lenny's success is a direct result of conquering whatever influence the Wilmington Tennis Association and others had and succeeding in spite of it.

When Lenny kept facing roadblocks, I encouraged him to go back to Knoxville. He said, "Mr. Rountree, I'm not going to let these people prevent me from making every effort of which I'm able to bring the kind of tennis dedication and discipline to youngsters that I know to be helpful." Through all of it he persevered, and he has helped hundreds of kids.

This community had a wonderful opportunity to allow a private person with talent and with joy and with utmost belief in this community to become a real leader, and turned him down until he made immense personal sacrifice to make it happen anyway. Lenny placed plenty of opposition from the white community in Wilmington, but also there isn't a single black person in this community wo has stepped up and really helped Lenny as he should. None.

If I believe it to be the truth, I'm old enough to say it, and I'll own up to it. But there has not been a person who has been willing to put his life and money on the line for the young, unappreciated disenfranchised youngsters in this community in my lifetime like Lenny Simpson.

CAROLYN MCLEMORE

With Lenny and I both being from Wilmington, I have followed his career since a child. I was so proud of his achievements breaking into tennis. He proved to everyone that anything is possible if you set your mind to it, regardless of race or background. He didn't let society dictate his life; instead, he took the bull by the horns and achieved greatness. Many years later, my husband and I were blessed by being introduced to Lenny and Jo Ann. We loved Lenny's vision for the foundation in helping underprivileged children learn the sport of tennis, and have access to tutoring, educational programs, and information about nutrition.

Dave and I wanted to help in any way possible to see the foundation succeed. We were so happy to be involved in the restoration of 1406 Orange Street. Dave and I were also blessed to have the opportunity to travel with Lenny, Jo Ann, and the One Love kids to the US Open and Wimbledon. We loved seeing the children's expressions as they saw these places for the first time. We were so grateful to be a part of this once-in-a-lifetime experience for the children. Throughout our travels with Lenny and Jo Ann, Dave and I bonded an unbreakable friendship with them.

Lenny's upbeat, motivating talks and prayers kept Dave fighting for his life against cancer. He kept Dave in line and pushing during physical therapy, as much as Dave hated physical therapy. The nurses were so grateful for Lenny. When the end was inevitable, Lenny and Jo Ann were at our house several times a week to pray with us. This was very comforting and appreciated by us. We will be forever grateful to Lenny and Jo Ann for letting us be a part of their lives. Even though Dave is no longer with us physically, he is here in spirit, and I will continue to support the foundation as Dave wished. I love you both so much and wish you all of the best. Congratulations on the book!

BERTHA BOYKIN TODD

I came to Wilmington from Durham in the fall of 1952 to become employed by the New Hanover County Board of Education and became friends with Lenny's mother, who was also in the school system. We were in a couple of organizations together and we also belonged to the same Presbyterian church. She kept me informed about both of her children. Lendward was away at the time, and I followed his tennis career as he played and received awards.

Then he and Jo Ann decided to move to Wilmington because he had this vision of developing One Love, which was to teach young boys and girls about tennis. He decided to form this nonprofit agency to train and help children, and during Covid he extended it to working with the parents as well as gathering food for the community.

I have always been interested in young folk of every hue who needed help in one way or another. In fact, I have many adopted sons and daughters of every hue. My hope, my faith has always been in the younger generation. I admire Lenny and Jo Ann for giving their time and their talents in working with the young boys and girls. He has taken them to many regional and national tennis programs on the funds that he and Jo Ann raised. So any time I see Lenny and his wife working with the community, I try to lend support in any way I can.

CIERRA BURDICK

I was introduced to Mr. Lenny and Ms. Jo Ann by Kevin Whitted during my freshman year at Tennessee. I still remember my very first dinner with the Simpson family—there was an instant connection. Mr. Lenny and Ms. Jo Ann quickly took me under their wing as if I was one of their own. It wasn't long before I was introducing them to my teammates as "My Knoxville family." They came to countless Lady Vol games to cheer and support. And about once a week I would go to their house to get away from the everyday stress of being a Division I student-athlete. The Simpsons' household was my safe haven. Going there to eat a home cooked meal, to sit in front of the fireplace, and to laugh until my core ached — those are some of my fondest memories from college.

I think one of Mr. Lenny's greatest qualities is his selflessness. He is always motivated by a greater cause and purpose. It's NEVER about him. When Mr. Lenny was playing, he knew he carried a heavy weight on his shoulders because of the color of his skin. But that weight served as his motivation. He wanted to see the black community afforded the same opportunity as their white counterparts. He wanted to continue to push black tennis forward just as he had witnessed Dr. Eaton, Dr. Johnson, Althea Gibson, and Arthur Ashe do before him. Every time he laced up his sneakers and picked up his racket, it was about creating more opportunities for the disadvantaged. Mr. Lenny's "Why?" has always been about something bigger than himself. And that's why he's accomplished all that he's accomplished.

As great of a player as Mr. Lenny was, it would be doing his legacy an injustice to solely talk about his playing accomplishments. The awards, the championships, and the rankings can all be recorded and measured. But what cannot be measured is the impact and influence Mr. Lenny has had as a mentor, advocate, and leader for at-risk youth. When reflecting on Mr. Lenny's legacy, it's important to celebrate the wins both on and off the tennis court. I, like the many kids of One Love Tennis, have directly benefited from Mr. Lenny's love and wisdom. His support and encouragement continue to be instrumental in my professional career today. That initial commitment to a greater purpose has touched countless lives, and Mr. Lenny's legacy will continue to have a ripple effect for years to come.

INZA WALSTON

I met Lenny during a luncheon at The City Club. I grew up in Wilson and my first tennis teacher, Tom Parham, was giving a lecture and I had not seen him in years. Tom asked Lenny to make some comments on the lack of diversity in college tennis (Tom had led ACC and Elon College to national championships) and I was very impressed with Lenny's thoughts. He also talked about his One Love program at the MLK center. I was VERY interested in what he was doing with and for these young children through tennis. I live on 5th Street and I told Lenny I was going to walk down the next day and help at 8th and Ann—I did and it was one of the BEST things I have ever done in my life.

I feel as if Lenny's main legacy in tennis is "coming home." Yes, his tennis abilities were world-class and had early injuries not come into play there's no telling how far he would have gone as a professional. He is a man, (along with Jo Ann,) who followed his heart and his faith and did not forget people that shaped him in his youth. He came home to pay tribute to them.

The love, discipline, respect, hard work, team work and skill Lenny used to accomplish this with a lot of children was amazing! Lenny truly doesn't hear the word "No," plain and simple. I am thankful for my ten-year connection to

One Love, Lenny and Jo Ann and all the great folks I have met through this organization.

HARRY KRALY

Lenny and I met on a tennis court in, maybe, the summer of 1969, playing in a tournament in Wilmington. He beat me, but I came off the court thinking what a nice guy he was. When he returned to Wilmington to start One Love Tennis, we reconnected and have cultivated a friendship over the years. We have had some very candid conversions about some very sensitive subjects. I appreciate and respect his honesty, forthrightness, and his point of view.

Lenny is tenacious, persistent and quick to stand up for what he believes. He is driven by faith and what he thinks is right. One Love is a great example of these traits. Lenny did not and has not allowed obstacles to stand in his way, either as a player or in developing the One Love organization. One Love is an extension of Lenny's youth development experience that helped shape him into the person he is today. He wants to pass those virtues, values, and character development on to other generations.

Lenny's accomplishments as a world-class tennis player put him in an elite field of tennis players. To put this in perspective, if you were to measure his tennis accomplishments in financial terms, he would be a billionaire. This has been acknowledged by his being inducted into the Southern Tennis Hall of Fame, the NC Tennis Hall of Fame and the Wilmington Athletic Hall of Fame, all richly deserved.

JANET GAINO

I have produced the video biographies for the Greater Wilmington Sports Hall of Fame since 2006. Lenny was inducted in 2012 and although we had communicated by phone, we did not meet until the end of the evening of the ceremony, after his induction and he had seen the video for the first time. This is before Lenny had decided to return to Wilmington, and I like to believe that event and that short video definitely helped move him in that direction. I'll never forget that night when we met; he so enthusiastically told me that we were going to work together and that I would help him with great things. And much to my surprise, we did and I have!

I was very much involved in the formation of One Love Tennis as a founding board member, and for many years I strove to learn and help tell and promote the story of Lenny Simpson and One Love Tennis. To say that Lenny and Jo Ann Simpson are my friends is an understatement. I love them dearly. Lenny is one of a kind! He has so many qualities... He is tenacious, persuasive, speaks from the heart, tough, kind and he loves the Lord!

From an early age, Lenny was touched and mentored by the amazing black trailblazing tennis legends in this book. He is a visionary who never forgot and always honored that historic tennis legacy. And he was determined that we would not forget either! That is why this book is so important...he has stories to tell that no one else can. Lenny has joined those legends as he touches and mentors young people, and to this day, he continues to give back–not only to the Wilmington Community but to the whole wide world of tennis.

CHARLIE RIVENBARK

I first met Lenny when I served on the Wilmington City Council, and I began a working relationship with him shortly thereafter. He told me if his dream of purchasing Dr. Eaton's home on Orange Street so I set up meetings with the owners and did a walkthrough at the house with him. I felt like I was stepping back in time to when he was a young boy and hanging out there on the backyard tennis court.

It was magical that first time, listening to him explain how this used to look and where everyone gathered and all the people he met there and what influence it had on his life!

I paid close attention to his facial expressions and the tone of his voice as he described his experiences with reverence. I knew from that day that he would most certainly succeed in his dream, and of course it has become a reality! I'm proud to know Lenny and feel honored that I had one scintilla of involvement in the process. Lenny is a giant to me!

LINDA UPPERMAN SMITH

Lenny and I grew up together here in Wilmington. He lived not far from me; I grew up at 14th and Queen, just a few blocks away from him. He had a passion for tennis as far back as I could remember. One day it seemed like he had just disappeared from Wilmington, and then we found out he had gone away to boarding school to play tennis. I did not closely follow his career, but I would ask his mom about him when I saw her.

Fast forward to early 2012. I had returned to Wilmington and received a phone call from Lenny. He was in town and wanted to connect after forty-plus years, and I invited him to dinner at my home that same night. When he rang the doorbell, I didn't see the skinny teenager I remembered from almost fifty years ago, but a mature man with the same big smile, booming laugh, and positive spirit. We spent the evening catching up. He shared his dreams about returning to Wilmington and teaching tennis to underserved youth in the community.

At the time I had a consulting business working with nonprofits and told him I could possibly assist. My suggestion was, however, to start with a for-profit business teaching tennis to become known in the community.

Lenny and I had different ideas as to how to accomplish his goals as we came to the process from different perspectives. It made for an interesting, animated relationship. After many discussions, a website was created, statistics were collected, interest in his project grew, and One Love Tennis was born. I served on his Advisory Committee and facilitated the meetings as well as assisted in One Love event planning and management. I worked with One Love Tennis until 2018.

The qualities that have allowed Lenny to accomplish so much in his life are his passion and love of tennis, his knowledge of the game, his desire to inspire others to learn the game, especially children, his positive outlook on life, his wisdom of choosing Jo Ann as his wife as she has stood by his side and supported him. Lenny brought his tennis career full circle. He went from being a black kid in Wilmington who experienced much racism as he began his tennis career, to returning to Wilmington, engaging with white men who he had formerly faced (and defeated) on the tennis court as a teen, and bringing them together to support bringing tennis to underserved youth in the community.

JOE CONWAY

I was introduced to Lenny through my work at the hospital as Director of Health Equity & Human Experience. Getting connected through the One Love program and Lenny's efforts was important in helping to address inequities within the community. Lenny is tenacious. He never gives up! He also has a strong character and believes in his purpose and mission in helping others become their best selves. Tennis is just a medium or method that he uses, but I believe he would be great at encouraging children and many others no matter the method used due to his stated purpose.

Lenny is a pro in every sense of the word. He is diligent, disciplined, and dedicated. He is also a coach, and the best kind, too, because he draws out the best, even when the 'coachee' doesn't realize their own potential.

CINDY DUCHARME

When I retired from teaching I was looking for something to do with inner-city kids, which had always been a passion of mine. I was introduced to Lenny. I was so in awe of him and his passion for what he wanted to do that I knew I wanted to be a part of it. The first year I helped with tennis (which I knew nothing about,) but he had other plans for me as we got to know each other. He wanted me to head up the academic enrichment part of One Love, and that's what I ended up doing. I have never met someone with such passion to make a difference in the lives of kids. He is a very determined, strong-willed man. He doesn't let anything get in his way from accomplishing what he wants in the best interest of kids. I know he had huge success in the tennis world but honestly what he has done for kids with character building and academics far surpasses that in my eyes. He is one of a kind!! There will never be another Lenny Simpson.

TOM COCHRAN

I met Lenny at church in Knoxville; he had a good voice and I was loud, and somehow it worked. Our families hit it off, and it has been that way for over thirty years. Like any great coach, Lenny enjoys the process of helping people improve. He and I were partners when he opened his own tennis center in Knoxville, and he was a natural promoter. He helped us win several national awards at Centre Court Racquet Club.

DAVID DOUGHERTY

My wife Kay and I retired to Wilmington in 2012. Before that, for twenty-one years I was a teacher at Episcopal High School in Virginia and for nineteen years I was the headmaster of The Hill School, a boarding school in Pennsylvania. When Kay and I arrived in Wilmington, we met Lenny Simpson, who as a boy had attended The Hill School from 1965-67. We were touched by his passion, his deep religious faith, and his tireless work for One Love Tennis. We knew immediately that he was genuine, "real."

We were inspired too by Lenny's story, beginning with his debt to Althea Gibson, the first African-American woman to play, let alone win the US Open and Wimbledon. Her life had touched me as a boy. But there was more.

- At 15 Lenny became the youngest male to play in the US Open.

- After Williston Middle School, he attended The Hill School and won the US Prep School Singles Championship. At The Hill his doubles partner was the future film director Oliver Stone.

- After graduating from East Tennessee State, where he captained the tennis team, he turned pro and qualified for Wimbledon.

- He became a teaching pro and co-owner of an indoor and outdoor tennis club in Knoxville, Tennessee, and for over thirty-seven years led programs for at-risk kids.

That's a powerful story. But the current chapter is the best – the call home in 2013 to help boys and girls, ages 6-12, most of them at-risk, aspire to the same kinds of ideals and hopefulness that have driven him, and to help his hometown meet the challenges of inner-city life that confront contemporary America.

From Wilmington to the US Open to Wimbledon and back again to Wilmington: It's an inspired story. That story is emotional. Lenny, supported by his wife Jo Ann, has wanted to help kids -- to learn tennis, work, and study hard, go to college, and live a good life. And the story is practical. Kids who learn a game like tennis and prepare for college will more likely resist the temptations of drugs and violence, to live healthy lives, to be positive leaders in the future.

Those are noble goals. And so Kay and I wanted to be a part of it. And we're glad – proud too – that we have helped Lenny achieve those goals. We're glad – proud too – that Lenny Simpson is our friend.

KAY DOUGHERTY

In 2012 the Simpsons returned to live, and the Doughertys to retire, in Wilmington. What we had in common was The Hill School, a boarding school located in Pottstown, Pa. Lenny had attended the Hill for two years in the 1960s, and David was the Headmaster of the School for nineteen years, both of us retiring in July 2012. So, we definitely knew about each other, but had never met. One afternoon shortly after moving here, I pulled up to a stoplight and in seconds noticed that the man in the car next to me was waving. Because I didn't know who he was, I sort of smiled to myself but didn't really acknowledge him. Then he held up a T-shirt that, in huge letters, spelled out THE HILL. The light dawned, and I rolled down my window and yelled, "Are you Lenny Simpson?" He, having seen The Hill School sticker on my car, yelled back, "Yes, are you

Kay Dougherty?" At that point, the light turned green, and we both drove away, promising we would get together soon.

Lenny Simpson has never lost sight of the values and principles he learned growing up: the importance of honor, hard work, and discipline. And woven throughout every decision and every step Lenny has ever taken is his faith that God is leading him down a certain path. Those of us fortunate enough to have watched Lenny in his work with kids (and I was one of the first group of academic coaches), have been witness to his love for them, and also his ability to teach and instill in them those values and principles, of his childhood, while coaching them both on the tennis court and in the classroom. He is a "no excuses" kind of person, and his kids, as he calls them, know that.

I believe Lenny's legacy within the sport of tennis has already been established, but more importantly to me—and I think Lenny—will be his legacy as an individual who was "called" to return to his hometown of Wilmington, NC, to create One Love Tennis. Its Mission Statement embodies Lenny's philosophy and approach to providing kids the same opportunities he had. "Our mission is to empower and inspire young people. Ages 5-12, especially those that are at risk, to positively change their lives through participation in a tennis and academic enrichment program." He continues to live that mission every day, and those kids who have been fortunate enough to have spent time with Lenny, will, for many years to come, benefit from the important lessons they learned from him. Now that's a legacy!

CHIP BOYD

I've been here for thirty-five years at Cheshire Academy; I came in as the boys varsity tennis coach. Cheshire Academy was a very small, somewhat struggling school at that time; I would not describe it that way now. I met Lenny at the 1994 bicentennial celebration of the school. I knew of Lenny, and I knew he was coming and I wanted to meet him. But I remember I walked into the area, and I was looking for him, and there was a group of about twenty guys around Lenny. He had been a three-sport athlete here; he was a player-coach of the tennis team even as a teenager. As I understood it all and it came into focus for me, it didn't surprise me that he was so popular with so many groups.

So I met Lenny, and we begin a conversation about one of his students possibly coming to Cheshire on a scholarship. Lenny's been here a number of times. When he was here presenting his film on Althea Gibson to the student body, I loved watching him interact with the students. The kids really responded to him, and many of them were hearing the name Althea Gibson perhaps for the first time, and they were astonished. One of my overriding impressions of Lenny is that he had dealt with He handles issues of race in tennis with so much grace and intelligence, sort of like his protégé Arthur Ashe. I think he was deeply impacted by Arthur, and I think Arthur would be very proud to see Lenny and his life.

I think that's part of his affection and loyalty to Cheshire Academy, I think that he and other people of color were able to find a foothold here, to have an experience here that gave them some strength and opportunity they might not have had elsewhere. He was even a trustee here for a couple of years. Lenny has just been very supportive to me. It's been a source of real happiness and pride to me that people like Lenny have had so much appreciation of me, when I'm just a high school coach. It's a real honor to me that he has respected my work at his school.

PRESTON ATHEY

I attended The Hill School in Pottstown, Pa. from 1963 to 1967. Lenny was one year behind me, but we overlapped for two years. As one of three African-Americans at the school in that era (out of 450 students) we all knew Lenny. He was popular with his classmates and admired by the upperclassmen because of his athletic prowess, both in basketball and tennis. Lenny left Hill after two years and attended and graduated from a different boarding school before heading off to college. But we invited him back fifty years later for a ceremony honoring the 1964 basketball team which went undefeated—beating both prep and high school teams as well as the Princeton and Penn freshman teams. At that dinner, Lenny told me that the two years at Hill were the most consequential years of his life. The teachers there gave him the confidence to power through adversity. His classmates affirmed him. While the academics were very rigorous, and life was pretty regimented, Lenny learned that he could do anything when he showed grit and determination. Hill prepared him for life, a lesson a lot of fourteen- and fifteen-year-olds never receive.

At that dinner, I learned about Lenny's dreams for the One Love Tennis program in Wilmington. He was just getting off the ground. I put him in touch with David and Kay Dougherty of Wilmington, encouraging Lenny to use their experience and connections to build a Board of Trustees. I know that relationship has borne great fruit. Lenny also gave a presentation to his classmates in the class of 1968 at their fiftieth reunion about his work with Wilmington kids. They were wowed by his efforts, and several joined in supporting the program.

Everyone makes a mark on the world during their lifetime. For some, it is limited by circumstances and compounded by a lack of vision. For some, it is limited by selfishness. When they are gone, it is reminiscent of President Lincoln's lines in the Gettysburg Address: "The world will little note, nor long remember" what they did, because it was of no consequence. But Lenny is different—he has poured out his love for a generation of kids at a time most people would have put their feet up and sat back. While the world may remember Lenny for his tennis exploits—for his breaking color barriers in his sport and for his professional teaching—he is honored now, and will be for years to come, because of his ministry to youth. That is Lenny's true mark on the world.

Lenny, we thank you and honor you. Well done, my friend.

PATRICK AND LISA BALLANTINE

My husband, Patrick, and I met Lenny at the Althea Gibson Tennis Complex while we were watching our son, Augie, play a tennis match during a Junior USTA Tournament. Augie was eight years old and playing in the Boys 10U division. Lenny gave us his card and let us know about some youth clinics he was offering. Augie enjoyed Lenny's clinics and lessons, and soon Lenny began coaching Augie's USTA Junior Team Tennis 10U Co-Ed Team. After a close regional defeat in year one, he took Augie's team to the national championship for the 10U age group the following year. Augie and Lenny have continued to have a close relationship on and off the court. Lenny is a one-of-a-kind role model, not just on the tennis court, but through his life experiences that he has shared with so many youth and their families. We consider Lenny and Jo Ann family, and Augie has benefited greatly from the coaching, mentoring, belief, and wisdom Lenny has shared with him.

Lenny's determination and competitive spirit have taken him far. His commanding voice paired with his kind heart make him a true leader. Lenny is a pioneer in so many aspects of tennis. His legacy started right here in

Wilmington, North Carolina. As a black boy growing up in a segregated society, young "Lendward" would probably not even have been exposed to the sport of tennis, but for the fact he lived right behind Dr. Hubert Eaton's property on 1406 Orange Street. The tennis court built by Dr. Eaton afforded Lenny the opportunity to be exposed to the sport of tennis and learn from role models and barrier breakers like Althea Gibson and Arthur Ashe.

Lenny's legacy in the sport of tennis is centered in his return to his roots, to provide the opportunities of tennis and education to this generation of youth through the One Love Tennis and Education program he founded. This legacy is furthered through the restoration of Dr. Eaton's historic home and tennis court. Giving back is a part of Lenny, just like his competitive spirit. Lenny and Jo Ann are a gift and treasure to the Wilmington community and beyond.

—◊—